AT A GLANCE

SOURDOUGH

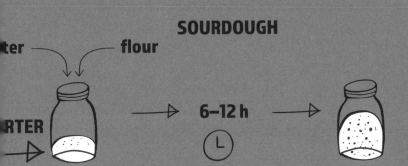

ter — flour

RTER

6–12 h (L)

FIRST RISE
ets of stretching after
the first 2 hours

PRESHAPING AND RESTING

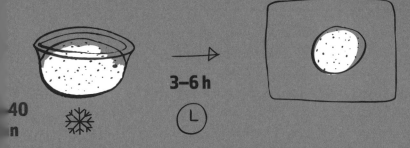

3–6 h (L)

40
n

❄

SCORING AND BAKING

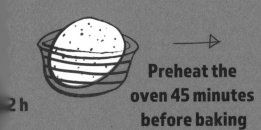

2 h

**Preheat the
oven 45 minutes
before baking**

see pages 78-114 for more information

SOURDOUGH MANIA

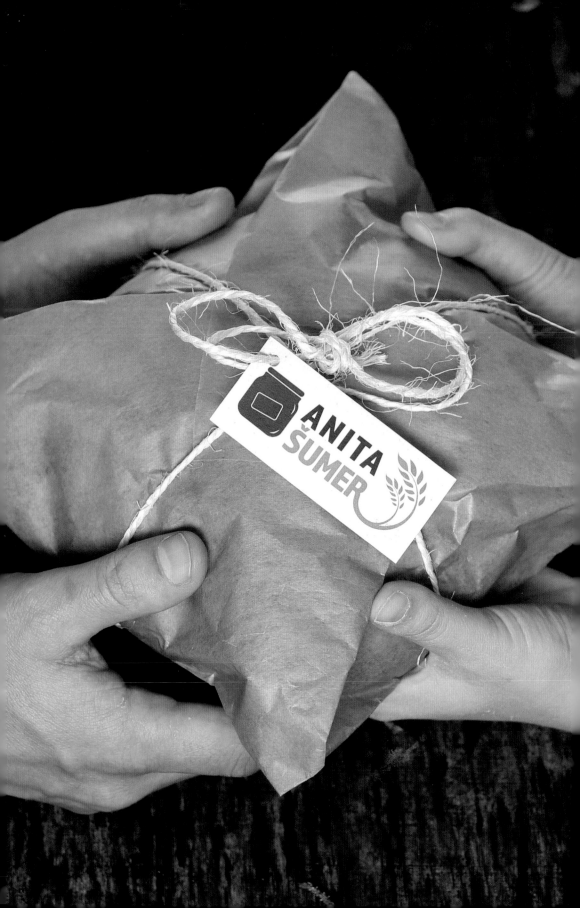

SOURDOUGH MANIA

THE COMPLETE GUIDE TO SOURDOUGH BAKING

Anita Šumer

Grub Street • London

Thank you!

I don't know where to start: there are so many people I would like to thank for their help and encouragement in baking and in creating my first book!

First of all, I wish to express a huge thank you to my late husband **Sašo**: it is thanks to you that I started baking bread and pastry. Thank you for all your advice and understanding, None of this would have been possible without your support and help. When I was having doubts, you quickly chased them away.

Thank you to my **family**, especially **my mother** and **grandmother**, who, from my earliest childhood, have awakened in me a love for cooking and baking.

From the bottom of my heart, I would also like to thank all my friends, who have collectively managed to eat large quantities of baked breads and pastries.

Thank you, dear **Barbara**, for all your help and support throughout my sourdough journey, as well as for all your friendly editorial advice.

Thank you, **Primož**, for the great photos, conversations, laughter and sessions dedicated to eating bread.

Thank you, dear **Manca**, for a wonderful redesign of this hugely successful book!

David, thank you for the section on cereals.

Thank you, **Miriam**, for your editing and advice.

I would also like to thank **Dr. Janez Bogataj** and **Brigita Rajšter** for their professional reading and critique of the book.

Thank you very much to all the supporters in the Facebook group **Drožomanija (sourdough_ mania)** – I believe that more and more of us are getting into the baking spirit every day.

Thank you to the **media** who have wished and still want to meet me. To all of us, spreading the love for sourdough baking around the world.

Thank you to my **sponsors**, Puratos, SPAR Slovenia, Miele Slovenia, Spilar's Mill and EKO365, companies that have made this publication possible through their support.

Together, we have succeeded in creating a unique book. Thank you very much!

Thanks to all the 'sourdough maniacs' and those of you who are about to become one.

A hearty and fragrant sourdough greeting,

contents

FROM SLOVENIA, SOURDOUGH MANIA SPREADS WORLDWIDE

The extraordinary success of the Slovenian first edition of this book is so remarkable that it has surprised everyone. Although we had secretly hoped the book would sell like hot cakes, we never imagined that it would have sold out in only three months after its release on 7 December 2017, or that we would sell almost 7,000 books so far. Thank you, dear sourdough lovers, for spreading *Sourdough Mania* together with us!

This is the third edition of *Sourdough Mania*, which has been updated and extended with new photography, two new chapters and an index.

Sourdough Mania is a project I started with the support and encouragement of my late husband Sašo. Sourdough baking had become a way of life for us that we loved to spread to others, and I will continue to do so in his memory. Together we organised more than 80 workshops attended by more than 1,000 participants, each time in a location carefully selected for its friendliness and warmth. These locations have contributed to making our sourdough workshops an unforgettable experience, and fortunately there is no shortage of them in our beautiful country.

We have also shared our knowledge abroad, where I am more and more often invited. My husband and I have travelled to several foreign countries: in September 2017 we accepted an invitation to Lisbon, in Portugal; in November of the same year we baked in Moscow; in January and February 2018 we took sourdough with us to Jamaica, in the Caribbean. In March I flew with my sourdough to Asia, first to Singapore and then Thailand. In April 2018 we proved that baking with sourdough can bring neighbours closer together: a workshop in Zagreb delighted the Croatians. After a brief rest, we flew to the UK and Stratford-upon-Avon, Shakespeare's birthplace, where we held a workshop. In September 2018, our journey took us to the Netherlands, where the Dutch got excited about sourdough in a workshop in Amsterdam.

Our journey took us to Paris in March 2019, where the *Sourdough Mania* book was exhibited at the UNESCO premises at the Gourmand World Summit.

September	November	January, February	March	Apri
2017	**2017**	**2018**	**2018**	
Portugal, Lisbon	Russia, Moscow	Caribbean, Jamaica	Asia, Singapore, Thailand	

Namely, the book *Sourdough Mania* was the Slovenian winner of the Gourmand World Cookbook Awards in two categories: 'Bread' and 'Charity Fundraising' and ranked among the nine best books for 2019 in these categories. In Macau, China, the book was voted the best bread book in the world and also received a charity fundraising prize (Europe).

In this short period of time, the number of my followers on Instagram (@ sourdough_mania) jumped to more than 80,000. And all the videos posted online (*Daily Mail*, Business Insider UK, UNILAD, BuzzFeed and others) had already exceeded 40 million views. At the same time, the number of sourdough enthusiasts in Slovenia increased significantly. I hope this is partially due to this easy-to-understand, richly illustrated book.

Our 'Drožomanija' (Sourdough_Mania) Facebook group now has more than 22,000 members! When I see the enthusiasm for making bread, sharing tips and helping each other, I am really proud because it fulfils the aim of the book: to spread the love and passion for this healthy baking style.

We decided not only to meet through virtual social networking but also to meet in person, to shake hands, to be able to exchange experiences and tips live. With the support of sponsors and partners, we organised the first Slovenian meeting for sourdough enthusiasts on 12 October 2019 in Mislinja, in Carinthia, and about 500 people participated in this event. The whole day was dedicated to sourdough, with expert lectures presented by Karl de Smedt from the Puratos company and Brigita Rajšter from the Slovenj Gradec Carinthian Regional Museum, a demonstration of decoration with Morgan Clementson, a short documentary *The Forgotten Recipe* by JRVisuals production company, and stalls with baking products and ingredients. We were pleasantly surprised by the response from the visitors, which gives us hope that this meeting will become traditional.

More and more people are paying attention to the bread they eat. So invite your friends, acquaintances and relatives, gift them a loaf of bread and share the sourdough with them so that the enthusiasm for sourdough will win them over too! By sharing this knowledge about the quality of sourdough, we ensure its wide dissemination.

Your baker,
Anita Šumer

| 18 | April | 2018 | September | 2018 | March | 2019 | June, July | 2019 |

| atia, greb | England, Stratford-upon-Avon | Netherlands, Amsterdam | France, Paris | China, Macao |

IT'S NOT THE FLOUR THAT MAKES BREAD, IT'S THE HAND!

This very precise Slovenian proverb simply confirms that making bread requires knowledge. If it is not flour that makes bread but the hand, it means that the hand is guided by knowledge. And it is precisely this knowledge that has enabled our ancestors to make bread. The more we look back to our distant historical past, the more unknowns come to light, even about the food we today refer to as bread. It is now generally accepted that the oldest bread was made of only flour and water. Some researchers consider, for example, the flat, essentially round, yeast-free Slovenian flat bread known as *mlinci* as one of the oldest methods for making and shaping bread. Yeast, or specifically brewer's or baker's yeast, brought about a new development in bread and bakery culture much later, and began to dominate from the second half of the 19th century.

Before the spread of yeast, housewives used a sourdough starter, which they prepared themselves from various ingredients and in different ways. There were also differences in the naming of this leavening agent. It was mostly used when making a new batch by incorporating small dough pieces into the ingredients. Where the financial situation allowed, housewives prepared bread once a week, making enough dough to last until the following week. The starter made it possible to ferment the dough. It had to be prepared at the beginning of the first batch as well as during all the subsequent batches, with a piece taken from the previous dough and formed into a small ball that was dried and added to the next batch of dough.

One of the oldest ways to prepare a sourdough starter requires only flour and water. It was often made from millet flour, which was stirred into grape must when it was fermenting. Millet or maize flour was also mixed with wine to make a leavening agent. In some places, flour and hops were mixed. Individual housewives also made a leaven and sold it door to door. In particular, leaven from the Gorenjska region, which was purchased by Slovenian housewives in Trieste in the 1880s, was appreciated. It was imported to Trieste from Kranj and was also known as 'fresh' yeast. Of course, during this time, some parts of the Gorenjska region had completely abandoned the use of sourdough starters for bread making and used only brewer's yeast. Sourdough use could have an 'archaic' side: women were only allowed to use spring water for its preparation when drawn at the precise moment that the bells rang for morning Mass at Pentecost, for example. In Dolenjska it was thought that when bread was poorly risen, water drops from a spinning milling wheel would help.

This is all just a tiny glimpse of the great story of bread and, above all, the knowledge for its preparation.

These testimonials are part of the cultural heritage that we are returning to today. They provide us with lots of useful information that can be beneficial for our modern life, a healthy diet, different, more natural flavours and much more.

When studying these different historical periods and learning about the everyday life and festivals of different social groups, it's important that we do not try to act like we're 'in a museum': in other words, we shouldn't try to copy our heritage but to 'understand' it, which can lead to many new and creative solutions. We shouldn't be making bread the 'old-fashioned way', but we should use old-fashioned methods to open up modern creative possibilities in the nutrition field. After all, this book by Anita Šumer confirms that the use of sourdough lends itself to different types of breads, bakes and pastries. From this perspective, the book represents a challenge to our contemporary efforts in nutrition. The reference to cultural heritage contributes to local and regional recognition and identity, now and in the future.

Prof. Dr. Janez Bogataj
Ethnologist
University of Ljubljana

BREAD, A GIFT FROM GOD

Sourdough Mania is a heartfelt cookbook about Anita Šumer's passion for sourdough baking. It is an endearing testimony to the return to the original culinary tradition of baking rye bread with sourdough, which is typical of Carinthia. She enthusiastically introduces new ways of using sourdough to recipes for well-known dishes, giving new life to their flavour.

'Bread is a gift from God', our distant ancestors used to say, who by treating it with respect, showed regard for their work. In a traditional agricultural home, the loaves of bread were laid out on the Christmas table to reflect the peasants' efforts in growing grain and producing flour. At Ojstrica and Strojna villages and elsewhere, anise was always added to rye bread for flavour, while in Libelice village, anise was only added to the 'table bread' that was baked at Christmas.

Over the centuries, with fluctuations between periods of abundance and scarcity, it became clear that bread on the table was not a commodity to be taken for granted, dependent solely on the effort put into it. Members of the agricultural community believed in the existence of a 'higher force' and generously devoted their efforts to the greater good of Creation. Just a few decades ago, there were religious processions held in green fields of young grain on the feast of Corpus Christi to protect the crops from calamities and pray for a good harvest. Full granaries were the only guarantee that families would not starve.

A loaf of rye bread was once a means of payment. The sacristan of the St Magdalene na Vratih church was tasked with ringing the bells if there was an approaching storm, as the sound of bells was supposed to disperse the clouds and thus prevent a violent storm. Once a year, from each farm within hearing of the church bells, he was given a loaf of rye bread to pay for 'the defence against the storm'.

In Ojstrica, the village above Dravograd, a loaf of rye bread paid for a neighbour's help in transporting manure. As a reward, the mistress of the house distributed a loaf or a large piece of rye bread and cooked dried meat to the servants and maids when they were on holiday from Christmas to New Year's Day.

Many everyday tasks have been associated with the respect and veneration of rye bread. As a rule, the bread never ran out. it was usually stored in a drawer in the dining table with a knife placed next to it. Whoever was hungry could cut himself a piece of bread. Guests were given a loaf of rye bread and a knife and invited to cut as much as they wished. A piece of bread cut from a loaf had a triangular shape like a piece of cake. The only drink offered with the rye bread was fermented apple juice.

A loaf of bread was never placed 'on its back', but always carefully placed on the table or in the drawer.

If someone put a knife on the bread, it meant that the bread could run out.

The sliced side of the bread was never allowed to face the door, believing that the bread could escape through it. Before the bread was cut, a cross mark was made with the knife tip on the back of the loaf.

Traditional rye bread always takes the form of a boule and weighs between three and four kilograms. Making bread by hand requires certain knowledge, skills and physical abilities. The day before baking, a wooden dough trough is brought into the kitchen, and all of the flour is placed into it to bring it to room temperature. At the same time, the starter is also added. The next day, the dough is kneaded with the starter. In Libelice it is customary to say: 'The bread will be like the starter. If you knead it softly, the bread will be soft and vice versa.'

The bread was usually made by the mistress of the house. When younger girls were at home, they helped to knead the dough and learned baking skills from their elders. These older women's experience was also welcomed in heating and ensuring the correct temperature of the oven.

The sign of a blessing is still often practised during bread making. The right hand makes the sign of the cross while the litany 'Holy Cross of God' is recited before beginning the work, kneading the dough, leaving the dough to rise, shaping the loaves and putting it into the oven.

In Šentanel village, the triangular sign of the Holy Trinity is still stamped on the bread before it is baked. This act, as well as the blessings with the cross, certainly dates back to pre-Christian agricultural cultures.

Bread making is still a special family event that also brings joy to children. Mothers have always known that the smell of freshly baked bread stimulated their desire for it. In Libelice, Striezeln and Ojstrica villages, they used to comfort their children with specially baked 'trenta' buns, and elsewhere with white bread. For the trenta, a small piece of rye dough was rolled up and spread with soured cream, scattered with cumin and salt and then baked in the oven. Striezel, or plaits, were also spread with soured cream, scattered with fresh tarragon or chives and plaited into a long loaf.

It is said that 'You only need to make a sourdough starter once, then you have it forever.' When a farm is passed on, 'the young' also inherited the sourdough starter or the leftover dried dough from the last baking batch. For the housewife, the 'loss' of the sourdough starter through neglect was one of the greater embarrassments.The sourdough starter was preserved from baking to baking and passed on from one generation to the next.

With its active substances, it represented a connection between living family members and their ancestors.

To complete the circle of her passion, Anita Šumer registered her own sourdough starter, which she affectionately calls Rudl, with the Puratos Belgium online sourdough library.

Due to the inherent scientific nature of the subject of sourdough, her book is more than welcome. Anita has pioneered the way for the geographical protection of Carinthian rye bread as a first-class culinary product, which we have been given to preserve for posterity. We hope that the Carinthian farmers who continue to bake rye bread with their own starters will also embrace a passion for sourdough. After all, they are the custodians of the great culinary tradition of our cultural heritage.

The path to the future with respect for tradition!

Brigita Rajšter, Carinthian Regional Museum

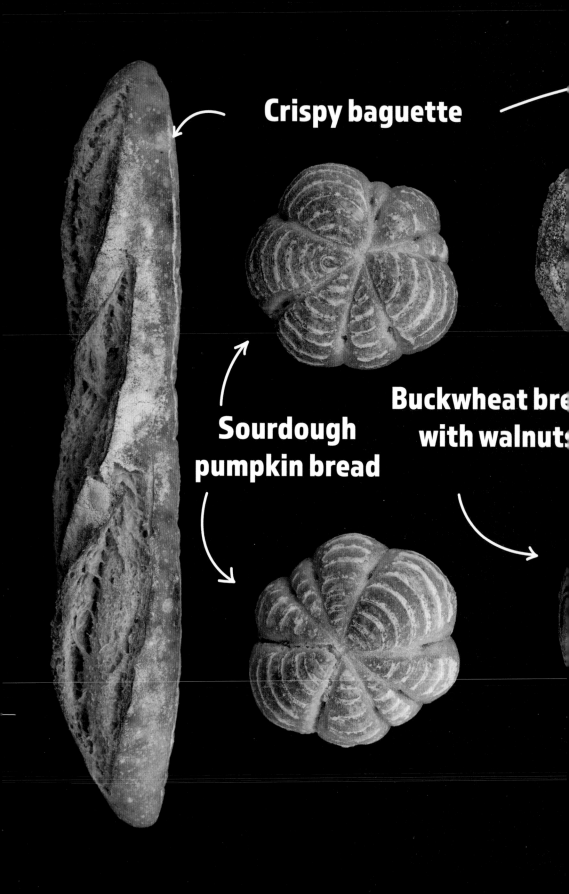

Crispy baguette

Sourdough pumpkin bread

Buckwheat bre with walnut

Yellow corn bread

introduction

Who would have thought that a simple mixture of flour and water could be turned into bread?

Do you remember back in our school days when we used a mixture like that to glue paper? I remember them perfectly. At the time I would never have dreamed that this mixture of flour and water would bubble and come to life when warmed up, or that it could be kneaded and baked. This ancient ingredient for leavening bread was named sourdough. But this sour name, I admit, can be a bit misleading, and I'm not a big fan of it. Especially since, when done right, sourdough isn't sour or hard at all, but soft and scrumptious in the centre. But sourdough by any other name would smell just as sweet, so let's stick to the established terminology.

My interest in sourdough goes back to eight years ago, when my late husband Sašo had his gallbladder removed and could no longer eat ordinary bread made with baker's yeast. This was why I started researching how to make a bread that he could eat but that also neither he nor I could resist. Since 2012, I have been reading many books, websites, blogs and articles, but I've learned mostly from baking myself. The more bread I baked, the better I got. I even began baking up to three times a week! The beginnings were vastly different than my products today: too flat and sour. But I didn't discard anything – my husband and I ate every last crumb. Using a starter has taught me that delicious and nutritious bread can be baked with only three ingredients: flour, water and salt – plus, of course, all the energy and love I put into the dough. This kind of baking has also taught me how to plan, be patient and adapt. This book is intended as a simple introduction to the world of baking with sourdough, so don't let the numbers mislead you. When baking bread, forget about the clock. Instead follow the dough with all your senses: touch it, smell it, observe how it changes.

You might be asking yourself why should you begin baking in this old-fashioned way, one that takes up so much time and energy? Keep reading, as I hope this book will clear up some of the myths about well-baked, delicious bread that's just like our grandmothers used to make. And not just bread, but also other specialities too! All you need is a little planning and organisation to make baking part of your daily routine. The other elements are a lot of patience, a bit of time to master it and love – and you will surely succeed. Don't let a burnt or flat loaf overwhelm you – we've all been there, and sometimes I still don't manage to make the perfect loaf. It happens to everyone and isn't a reason to give up. It should just serve as greater motivation to keep trying until you get it right. The reward is a temptingly delicious, wonderfully fragrant and nutritious loaf of bread.

Let me also use this introduction to present you to 'Rudl': that's the name I've given to my starter. It has been with me from the very beginning and has become an indispensable part of my baking activities. Rudl excels at both bread and sweet treats.

Ever since I started baking with a starter, I have been sharing this love and passion with everyone around me. I see my mission as spreading this nutritious and delicious form of baking throughout my home country of Slovenia and beyond its borders to the rest of the world. So, I invite you to join me on this amazing and delicious sourdough journey. But beware: sourdough is addictive. It won't let me go, and there's a good chance it could win you over too!

from grain
to starter

Without flour, there is no bread... but what exactly is flour made of? Are all cereals the same or are they divided into separate categories? In this chapter, I will introduce you to the most commonly used plants whose grains and seeds are used to make flour. I will also give you an overview of the different types and qualities of flour before we start making bread together.

TYPES OF GRAINS

According to morphological and biological characteristics, there is a distinction between types of true cereal grains and also pseudo-cereal grains. True cereals include wheat, rye, barley and oats. This group also includes millet-type cereals such as maize (corn), millet, sorghum and rice. The first group of true cereals mentioned here are unusual in that they do not require high temperatures to grow, whereas the latter millet-type cereals are more demanding when it comes to heat, especially in the final stages of plant development. Due to these characteristics, true cereals are known as either moderate climate zone grains or as warm climate zone grains if the millet type.

Also worth mentioning are buckwheat, quinoa and amaranth, although in principle they are not considered to be cereals because of their morphological characteristics. This group is referred to as pseudo-cereals.

More recently, there has been increasing reference to 'ancient grains'. They include cultivated wheat species such as spelt, whose grains are surrounded by a husk or ball. These cereals are the genetic ancestors of the higher-yielding and highly hybridised cereal varieties. For example, spelt is the distant ancestor of common (or soft) wheat. Due to their properties, archaic cereals are more suitable for organic farming.

TRUE CEREALS

WHEAT (*Triticum* sp.) is an annual plant belonging to the Poaceae family (grasses). According to a recently discovered source, wheat originated in the plain region of the Anatolian peninsula of Turkey (the so-called Fertile Crescent region). It has been cultivated since 9000 BC. It has also been cultivated in Mesopotamia and Syria since 3000 BC. Wheat production had a significant impact on the lives of people in ancient Egypt. The genus *Triticum* is composed of wild and cultivated species, and these differ in the number of chromosomes. They are known as diploid, tetraploid and hexaploid wheats. Included here are the types and varieties of wheat most commonly used in baking.

COMMON WHEAT (hexaploid) (*Triticum aestivum* L. subsp. *aestivum*) is the most common wheat species in the world. Its flowers are grouped in an inflorescence called an ear, in which about 40 bare seeds develop. Compared to other cereals, it provides yields that allow the production of many cereal products containing 8–14 per cent protein. Because it contains a sticky substance known as gluten, it is ideal for making bread and other pastries.

OTHER TYPES OF WHEAT are einkorn spelt (diploid), emmer spelt (tetraploid and hexaploid) and common spelt (hexaploid). Genetically, these species differ in the number of chromosomes as well as morphologically by the number of grains in a ear.

An important morphological difference between common wheat and spelt is that in the threshing of common wheat, the grain just falls out of the chaff, while the spelt grain remains in the chaff. The two varieties also differ in the number of grains in the ear.

EINKORN SPELT (*Triticum monococcum* L.) usually has only one grain per ear (it is also known as one-grain spelt), which is not bare at harvest but wrapped in husks. Its ancestor was used in the Palaeolithic period. Until the 20th century it was cultivated in the Caucasus, the Mediterranean and north-western Europe. It was the first cultivated cereal in the Balkans. In the 21st century it has become intensely cultivated in the United States.

EMMER SPELT (*Triticum dicoccum*), also called starch wheat, has the same origin as the other spelts listed here. It was already in cultivation by the Palaeolithic period. It was cultivated in the Middle East, Europe and North Africa during the Stone Age and Bronze Age. In the 19th century, it was produced on a large scale, particularly in Russia. Today it is an important crop in Ethiopia and India, and it is grown in Europe in Italy (it. *emmer* or *farro*). The spikelet of this wheat has two well-developed husked grains.

SPELT (*Triticum spelta* L.), the most commonly used wheat cereal in organic farming, typically develops two grains per ear. When compared to common wheat, spelt has less grains per ear, but they are larger. Initially, common spelt was not one of the major cereals in the region where wheat originated (Fertile Crescent). Its true value has been recognised in its ability to adapt to cold, wet climates. It could therefore be cultivated in the North-western Alps region, and it was brought to Central Europe in the 4th century BC. After the Second World War, its production declined in Europe, mainly due to the lower yield per hectare compared to common wheat. More recently, due to its simplicity and adaptability to growing conditions, it has become a major bread-making cereal.

Durum wheat

Einkorn Wheat

Wheat

KHORASAN (*Triticum turanicum Jakubz.*) is a tetraploid wheat species. This type of wheat is known in the United States under the trademark 'Kamut', and its reproduction and marketing is only permitted in the United States by KANA (The Kamut Association of North America) and in Europe by KAE (Kamut Association of Europe). According to some American sources, Kamut is a wheat that stems from 36 grains imported from Egypt.

DURUM WHEAT (*Triticum durum* Desf.) belongs to the hexaploid wheat family. By its prevalence of production it comes in second, only behind common wheat. It thrives in hot summer areas (in the Mediterranean, North Africa, Central America and the southern United States). The high protein content in its flour makes it ideal for making pasta.

RYE (*Secale cereale* L.) originates in the Middle East. The ancient peoples (Egyptians, Sumerians, Assyrians, Babylonians, Chinese and Greeks) did not know rye; only the Romans mentioned it in written sources. It was brought to Europe as a weed between wheat and barley. Rye was cultivated in northern Germany from 800–500 years BC and then by the Celts. The Slavs cultivated it in the area of their original homeland (part of south-western Europe between the Vistula and the Dnieper), which was later taken over by Germans during their migration to the west of Europe. Until the Second World War, rye was an important European grain, especially in colder climates and in areas 1,000 metres above sea level. It is also produced for animal feed and industrial purposes. Russia, Poland, Germany, Belarus and Ukraine are the main producers of rye.

TRITICALE (*Triticosecale* Wittm. & Camus) is a hybrid (amphiploid) cereal that was created by artificially crossing rye and wheat. In 1875, the Scottish botanist Alexander Stephen Wilson first tried hybridising wheat and rye, but his hybrids were sterile. The first fertile grains were made a bit later by the German researcher Rimpau. Initially, triticale was merely a botanical curiosity, but in recent decades it has become increasingly popular in cereal production. Some breeders call triticale the grain of the future as it can be grown in areas not suitable for wheat. The advantages of triticale over other cereals include its resistance to low temperatures and the possibility of larger harvests. Triticale does not yet have a significant place in human nutrition due to its low gluten content. It is mainly grown in Poland, Russia, Germany, the United States, France, Bulgaria, the United Kingdom and South Africa.

BARLEY (*Hordeum vulgare* L.) is one of the first cultivated cereals and is an important cornerstone in the development of civilisation in the Middle East. It is native to Asia (six-row barley) and Africa (two-row barley). It was cultivated in Egypt 7,000 years ago. In ancient Greece and Rome, barley bread was the bread of poor Roman citizens and soldiers. Gladiators also ate barley, which is why they were nicknamed 'barleymen'.

As with spelt, there are several known varieties of barley, which differ in the number of rows of grains in an ear. In industrial processing, it is mostly used to produce malt for beer, for the production of alcohol and starch, and for the production of whisky.

OATS (*Avena sativa* L.) is native to South East Asia. The ancient Egyptians did not know oats. The Greeks (4th century BC) and the Romans (6th century BC) only cultivated oats for animal feed. In Europe, oats were grown by the Celts, Germanic tribes (1700–1500 BC) and later by the Slavs, who only ate bread made from oat flour. Oat bread is still eaten today, mainly in Scotland and Norway. In the Middle Ages, oats were the most important grain in Europe, but since the mid-20th century its production has declined significantly. It has been replaced by wheat, barley and maize for their higher yields per hectare and due to the introduction of agricultural mechanisation. Oats production has continued in northern mountainous regions where climatic conditions do not allow the cultivation of conventional cereals.

MILLET-TYPE CEREALS

Along with wheat and barley, **MILLET** is one of the oldest cultivated cereals. Originally from Central Asia, it was grown in China in 10,000 BC. Millet is mentioned in ancient texts whenever they refer to wheat. The Romans enjoyed millet as porridge and baked bread (panis). It is one of the first cereals grown in Europe for human consumption.

In the millet family there are many plant genera and species that have small round seeds. The more commonly known teff (*Eragrostis tef* (Zucc.) Trotter.) also belongs to millet. Teff is becoming increasingly more popular in Europe. Even today, it is still the most important grain in Ethiopia.

RICE (*Oryza sativa* L.) is native to Asia and some cultivated species also come from Africa. It was being grown in China in 3000 BC. It was brought to Europe during the reign of Alexander the Great in the 4th century BC. Although the Greeks and Romans were aware of the grain, it was not an established ingredient in their homes. Arabs brought rice from Egypt to Europe through Spain in the 7th century, from where it spread to Italy. Among the rice subspecies, the most common are long-grain rice (*Oryza sativa* L. ssp. *Communis*) and short-grain (*Oryza sativa* L. ssp. *Brevis*). The rice grain is covered in a husk or chaff.

Wheat

Buckwheat

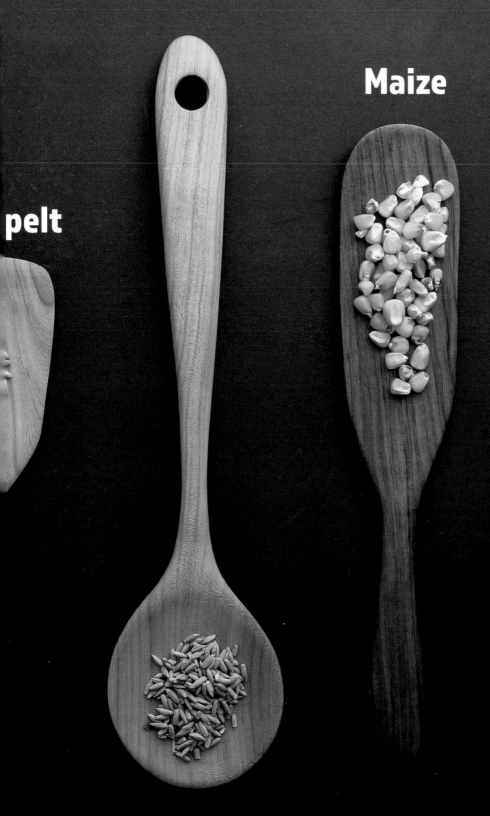

pelt

Maize

Rye

MAIZE (*Zea mays* L.) is the only cereal originating in the Americas (Mexico and Peru), where it has been grown since 4500 BC. The Mayans considered it a sacred plant, and the indigenous people of Mexico, the Incas and the Aztecs were familiar with it too. Maize (corn) was brought to Europe by Columbus' expedition (the first in 1492 or the second in 1494). From Spain it spread north and east. It was transported by the Venetians on their trade routes through the Mediterranean. The name corn (*kokoruz* in Turkish) was established in the 20th century by the Slavs. For milling into flour and semolina, a hard variety is the most suitable. Maize is still a staple in the Americas, Asia and Africa. Of all cereals, it offers the best yield and is the world's leading crop.

PSEUDO-CEREALS

BUCKWHEAT (*Fagopyrum esculentum* Moen.) is a dicotyledonous plant and belongs to the Polygonaceae (knotweed) family; it is therefore considered a pseudo-cereal. Originally from south-western China, it slowly spread to Bhutan, Nepal, India and Pakistan. Its capacity to thrive at altitudes above 3,000 metres, makes it an important crop in Bhutan and Nepal. Buckwheat was first mentioned in Europe in 1396. After the Second World War, buckwheat slowly declined in Europe in favour of higher yielding wheat, barley and maize.

Buckwheat seeds are triangular grains with different sharp and jagged edges, also called achenes. Buckwheat grain contains proteins of high nutritional value. Its amino acid composition meets our daily requirements. Compared to wheat, soya or meat, its protein is of higher quality. Due to the population's growing awareness about balanced nutrition and buckwheat quality, its production is increasing.

QUINOA (*Chenopodium quinoa* Willd.) is a lesser-known pseudo-cereal, originating from the Andes in South America, where it is still considered a very important crop today. It was cultivated 3,000 to 5,000 years ago by the indigenous American peoples, and was called 'mother grain' by the Incas. It was also cultivated in Germany during the First World War. Quinoa seeds contain a lot of protein, saponin, amino acids, natural antioxidants (vitamin E, alpha and gamma tocopherols), vitamins B2 and B6, folic acid, biotin and minerals. The seeds provide an ideal ratio of fat, starch and protein.

AMARANTH (*Amaranthus* sp.) is also a pseudo-cereal and is native to Mexico and South America. During the pre-Columbian American civilisations, it was an indispensable food source. It was being cultivated in Mexico in 4000 BC. For the Aztecs, amaranth was a staple food along with maize. Amaranth has a high protein content (12 to 18 per cent) and lysine (5 per cent), fats (7–8 per cent) and squalene (4.5 per cent), minerals and vitamins, fibre (4 per cent), colourants and lectins also carbohydrates, averaging 65 per cent (65 g per 100 g of grain).

COMPOSITION OF A GRAIN

Each cereal grain consists of a kernel (endosperm), a husk and a seed germ (cotyledon). The kernel is divided into two parts, the inner part or endosperm and the outer part or aleurone layer. Most starch and protein are hidden in the inner part, which makes up the largest part of the whole grain. The major constituents of the aleurone layer are soluble proteins, fibre (cellulose), vitamins, minerals and enzymes. The husk covers the grain and is full of fibre, vitamins, minerals, enzymes and some soluble proteins. The germ contains fats, soluble proteins, vitamins and enzymes in germ. (Horvat, 2010)

The chapter on cereal classification was created in collaboration with MSc. David Kranjc, B.Sc.agr.

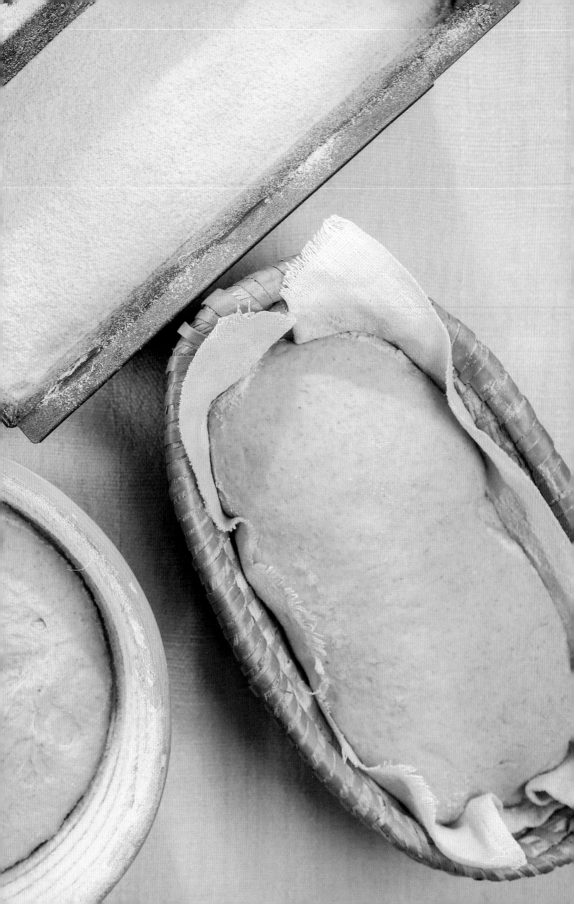

FLOUR BECOMES BREAD

From the true cereals and pseudo-cereals previously described, flour is obtained by grinding the grains on stone or steel millstones. 'From this flour shall come no bread' is a popular proverb. You have probably already discovered on your own that flour isn't just flour. The different types of flour can be divided into flour that can be used for making bread and flour that cannot be used on its own to make bread. A flour that can be used to make bread contains proteins that form gluten on contact with water, i.e. pentosans that swell in water. A non-leavening flour has very little or no protein in it. For a dough to rise well with one, it is necessary to mix it with a leavening flour or to blanch it to allow the starch to bind with water. Leavening flour is obtained by milling common wheat, rye, spelt and triticale. Non-leavening flour includes buckwheat, maize, millet, barley and gluten-free teff and rice flours. Oat flour, while gluten-free, contains another protein, avenin, which is similar to gluten.

WHAT'S HIDDEN IN FLOUR

Flour consists mainly of carbohydrates. Simple carbohydrates are called monosaccharides (e.g. glucose and fructose), and these bind to form compound or complex sugars (disaccharides) such as maltose and polysaccharides, most of which are starch. Starch consists of amylose and amylopectin. Because starch in its original form is inaccessible to yeasts, which feed on simple sugars, it needs help from enzymes, namely amylases, which convert compound sugars into simple sugars. When water is added to flour, it activates these enzymes to begin working and, thanks to the water, they can move around the dough.

Protein of different quantities and quality comes second. Some proteins are soluble in water, others make gluten when in contact with water. These two types of proteins are called glutenin and gliadin. Glutenin provides the elasticity and strength of a dough, gliadin provides stretchability and viscosity. When water is added to flour, glutenin and gliadin combine to gluten and chains, which in turn combine to form a glutinous mesh that traps the carbon dioxide produced by the yeast during fermentation. The higher the protein content, the greater the ability of the flour to absorb as much water as possible. Adding water to flour also activates the protease enzyme, which breaks down proteins.

In addition to carbohydrates and proteins, flour also contains minerals, vitamins, fats and fibre (cellulose).

In continental Europe, flour is classified by type. You may have seen the German type 405, 550 or 812 (or the French type 45, 55 or 80) and other markings on flour packaging and wondered what they mean. These numbers indicate how much ash (as a percentage) remains after the combustion of 100 grams of flour, which corresponds to the mineral content. Thus, after burning 100 grams of type 405 flour, 405 mg (or 0.405 per cent) of ash remains. The lower the flour type number, the fewer nutrients it contains.

Standard wheat flour types from common wheat:
- type 405 flour with up to 0.45 per cent ash
- type 550 four (similar to British plain flour), containing 0.55 per cent ash, high starch and low in protein, but of good quality and therefore with good baking properties
- type 812 flour (similar to British strong white bread flour) with 0.812 per cent ash has a higher protein percentage (around 11-13 per cent) containing more cellulose and fat, but with a higher nutritional value and is better suited to making bread
- type 1050 flour (similar to British brown flour) with 1.05 per cent ash and type 1600 (similar to British wholemeal flour) with 1.6 per cent ash contain many poor-quality proteins, husk and germ particles and, consequently, more vitamins, minerals and cellulose, and is therefore the most nutritious

Lower-grade wheat flour types have higher quality proteins (better gluten or glutinosity), so bread from such flour will rise better, with a better and more open crumb with larger holes. Higher-type flours, however, contain less high-quality protein but more nutrients. Therefore, bread from these types of flour will have a smaller volume and a more dense crumb, but it will also have a fuller and better taste.

As mentioned before, durum wheat is also suitable for making bread. Note that durum wheat semolina is not suitable for bread making; it is the flour that can be used to make bread dough. If you have a mill, you can grind semolina (It. *semola*) a second time at home. The coarse flour (It. *rimacinata semolina* – milled twice) can also be ground again to obtain a finer flour. For my part, I grind my own flour.

Manitoba flour is a special wheat flour with a high gluten-protein content. This flour can be mixed with other types of low-gluten flour to strengthen the dough.

In the UK, there is white plain flour (roughly corresponds to type 550), strong white bread flour (corresponds to type 812), brown flour (roughly corresponds to type 1050) and wholemeal flour (the same as German wholemeal flour). In Italy a distinction is made between type 00 (similar to 405), 0 (similar to 550), 1 (similar to 812), 2 (similar to 1050) and wholemeal flour. The designations do not completely correspond: the comparisons are meant as an approximate guide. Some of the types of flour available elsewhere in Europe are not typically sold in the UK such as the French type 45/German type 405 flour, which is a very fine flour. You can use the Italian type 00 flour found in some supermarkets, substitute it with white plain flour or search online for specialist bakery suppliers that sell Continental European flours.

It may be worth mentioning the difference between coarse meal and fine flour, which is simply in the size of the flour particles. The former has larger particles, the latter smaller.

Standard types of spelt flour:
- spelt flour type 630 – a flour comparable to white wheat flour
- wholemeal spelt flour, milled from the whole spelt grain

Although spelt contains more protein than wheat, the composition of these proteins is different and forms a poorer glutinosity. Spelt flour dough is more softer, but not as elastic as that made from wheat flour. Dough made only from spelt flour and without a mould, will sink easily and the bread will consequently be flat. You should therefore use less water for spelt flour (55–60 per cent) than for wheat flour.

Standard types of rye flour:
- type 185 rye flour
- type 997 rye flour
- types 115, 1370 and 1740 rye flour
- wholemeal rye flour

The gluten-forming proteins in rye are different from those in wheat, because rye contains mucilages called pentosans. These bind water and form a dough structure instead of a gluten mesh. This is why rye flour alone can be used to make bread, but the loaf will be flat and compact. In the case of rye flour, it is particularly important to use a sourdough starter in the preparation for making the dough, so the bread has a nice crumb.

NOTES FOR USING DIFFERENT FLOUR TYPES

The easiest flour to start baking with is undoubtedly type 550 (British white plain flour) or type 812 wheat flour (British strong flour). Use these two varieties separately a few times to help you learn the methods and techniques. Once you have a better understanding of baking, I recommend finding a good ratio between flour types and blending them so your bread will rise well, have a nice airy crumb and a good flavour. In the case of flour made from so-called ancient grains (einkorn, emmer, khorasan), barley, oats, maize or buckwheat, use up to 30 per cent of these type of flours. Blanch gluten-free flour before premxing so the starch will bind the water.

Mix wholemeal flour in a ratio of 50 per cent white wheat flour or a high-gluten flour to give a better volume and a nice crumb. In addition, the bread will be healthier and tastier because of the higher fibre content. Of course, these are just recommendations – try as many combinations as you can to master the whole process from kneading to baking. Also note that different types of flour absorb different amounts of water.

Whenever I can, I mill my own cereals (mainly wheat, spelt, einkorn, emmer) at home just before I make the dough. I use a KoMo Fidibus Classic stone mill, which I am very pleased with, because I can adjust the grinding setting, it does not overheat the flour and it grinds to the maximum possible fineness. Such freshly ground flour is the most nutritious and contains the most minerals and vitamins. What's more, the smell of freshly ground flour is intoxicating. If you grind flour at home, use the flour immediately after grinding it, within 24 hours at the latest. Otherwise, in my experience, it is better to let the flour rest for a while. You can also freeze the grain before grinding to reduce any overheating.

Spelt flour

Rye flour

White wheat flour

Wholemeal wheat flour

Buckwheat flour

BAKING PERCENTAGES EXPLAINED

Many recipes, especially international ones, contain percentage data, which means that all quantities are calculated based on the total amount of flour in the dough. To determine the weight of the other ingredients, each ingredient is weighed in relative proportion to the total weight of the flour. It is therefore easier to recalculate when writing or reading recipes if you want to bake with 1 kilogram or 500 grams, or maybe just 300 grams of flour. It makes it much easier to adjust the amount of ingredients to your own needs. As mentioned in the introduction, kitchen scales will become a good friend, especially for novice bakers. However, if you're not a fan of weighing, you can have a go without it.

EXAMPLE

RECIPE:
1 kg flour (e.g. 500 g white plain flour, 400 g strong white bread flour, 100 g rye)
600 g water
20 g salt
200 g starter

1 kg of flour is 100%.

600 g of water is 600 divided by 1,000 = 0.6 and 60%, respectively.

The amount of water or liquid in the dough is therefore 60%.

20 g of salt is 20 divided by 1,000 = 0.02 and 2%, respectively.

In general, the amount of salt in the dough is between 1.5 and 2%.

200 g of starter is 200 divided by 1,000 = 0.2 and 20%, respectively.

The recipe expressed as a percentage is therefore as follows:
100% flour (50% white plain flour, 40% strong white bread flour, 10% rye)
60% water
2% salt
20% starter

For a recipe with 400 g flour:

400 g flour (100%)
240 g water (60%)
8 g salt (2%)
80 g starter (20%)

40 g seeds (10%)

The recipes in this book are made with Continental flours in mind, so the readers in the UK and USA will need to adjust the water content as Continental European flours do not absorb as much water as British or American flours. So for UK and USA add perhaps 5-15 per cent more water than stated in the recipes. I recommend that you start with a lower percentage of water, about 60 per cent, or about 55 percent for spelt. Wholemeal flours and rye flour absorb water better, as they have a higher proportion of bran (cereal husks), so you can add more liquid to these types of flour, starting at 65 per cent. You can always add more water later.

SOURDOUGH, WHAT IS IT?

Many of us love a good cheese, bubbly beer, fine wines, dried meat, coffee and vanilla, sauerkraut, pickled turnips and many other such products. Microorganisms play an important role in all of these foods, just like in sourdough. Fermentation is one of the main ways of preserving and improving food, and it has played an important role in human development. The most delicious foods and drinks are often the result of fermentation.

Bacteria and yeasts live all around us, and also in us. The term 'microbiome' refers to all microorganisms that live in and on our body. Over the course of evolution, they have adapted to living with us, and we with them, so we live in perfect symbiosis. It's the same with sourdough. Sourdough is a natural leavening agent: a simple mixture of flour and water that, over time, begins to ferment spontaneously when warm. It really couldn't be simpler. From these two ingredients, you can make your own 'wild' yeast to completely replace baker's or brewer's yeast.

At first, I couldn't imagine it was even possible. Flour itself is abiotic, but if you add water – the source of life – that flour comes to life and begins to bubble and swell. It is full of various small organisms or microorganisms, which are not only present in the flour but also in the air. When I began my research into the nature of sourdough and the factors that make bread rise more than eight years ago, I found a lot of information online and in foreign literature. Many nations know of this leavening agent, only under different names. For example, the British and Americans call it 'sourdough starter' (it's an acidic dough) or simply 'starter' or 'sourdough', which corresponds to the German *Sauerteig*. The Italians use *lievito madre* (mother yeast), the French *levain* and the Russians *zakvaska* leaven, and the Spanish term is *masa madre* (mother dough), with part of the dough being reserved for the next bake. All these names have one thing in common: they are a mixture made of flour and water.

There are two different hypotheses to explain where and how humans discovered that they could use this fermented mixture for baking. The first sourdough dates back to 4000–3000 BC in Egypt. Legend has it that a woman forgot about some dough when making bread. Because the climate along the Nile is very humid and warm, the dough had risen sharply by the time she realised her mistake. She used it on the next kneading of dough and then baked it. The resulting bread was much softer than the earlier unleavened loaves.

And the baking process with a sourdough starter was discovered. The second version, however, says that the Egyptians, who were already familiar with brewing beer, began using its foam to raise bread.

Why is sourdough starter so important? Not only because it represents a cultural heritage that deserves to be preserved, but also because the products baked with sourdough are much more nutritious, easier to digest and more delicious.

THE SOURDOUGH PROCESS: FERMENTATION

WHAT HAPPENS IN THE STARTER TO MAKE DOUGH RISE?

Here is a simple explanation of the sourdough process: adding water to flour initiates spontaneous fermentation, since it activates the enzymes, lactic acid bacteria and wild yeasts present in the flour. These microorganisms are not only present in the flour, but also in the air, on our hands and everywhere else. Leavens are a microsystem in which lactic acid bacteria and enzymes begin to break down complex sugars into simple ones. These wild yeasts feed on these sugars, which in turn produces ethanol and carbon dioxide, which traps the gluten mesh and raises the dough.

Because lactic acid bacteria feed on maltose that wild yeast cannot digest, these microorganisms are also not in competition for the same type of food. As their name implies, lactic acid bacteria in this process secrete lactic acid as well as acetic acid, aromatic compounds, and sometimes carbon dioxide and ethanol. As this environment is acidic, only certain yeasts can thrive in it. An interesting fact: the ratio of lactic acid bacteria to wild yeast in sourdough is 100: 1.

However, if the sourdough becomes too acidic, it will have a pungent and sour smell that indicates it is running out of food. But the yeasts simply stop working, without dying off. Below, are solutions to this problem.

Fermentation and, consequently, the rising of dough are influenced by a number of factors:
- the amount of starter and its activity – if you add starter, the dough will rise faster; if you reduce, it will rise more slowly.
- heat: higher temperatures (of water and the environment) stimulate yeast and lactic acid bacteria activites; lower temperatures slow them down. Putting the dough in the refrigerator slows down the rising process, improving the taste of the dough. The ideal temperature for rising, which is suitable for both bacteria and yeasts, is 25–26°C/77–78°F.
- type of flour: if rye and wholemeal flour are used, the dough will rise faster, whereas with white flour it will rise slower.
- the amount of salt, which slows down the microorganisms' action while also enhancing the gluten, and the amount of sugar, which in small proportions (up to 5 per cent) stimulates the yeast and bacteria activities, but in greater proportions slows them down.

For comparison's sake, baker's or brewer's yeast contain only one yeast species, *Saccharomyces cerevisiae*, which has been selected to make the dough rise as quickly as possible. The concentration of this yeast is also much higher in baker's yeast than in sourdough, but there are many more species that thrive in an acidic environment. Since this baker's yeast raises dough in less than two hours, it quickly fills the mixture with carbon dioxide. It is precisely because of this rapid rise that some people may feel bloated and windy, as the lactic acid bacteria don't have time to do their job. And don't forget the distinctive smell of baker's yeast that results from its heavy use. I have noticed that I can tell whether bread was prepared with regular yeast by smelling it. It usually takes a while for taste buds to get used to bread made with sourdough – but once you do, you will no longer want to use any other leavening agent.

THE BENEFITS OF SOURDOUGH BAKES EXPLAINED

We now know what happens when sourdough ferments and why dough prepared with this leavening agent rises. This section explains why this method of baking is beneficial for our health and a good intestinal flora, and why it tastes incomparably better than bakes made with baker's yeast.

Easier digestibility

Bakery products prepared with sourdough are already partially digested, because much of the work is done for us by lactic acid bacteria and wild yeast, which partially breaks down the starch.

Reduced gluten content

The longer preparation and fermentation process makes wheat flour more easily digestible by reducing the amount of gluten since lactic acid bacteria break down gliadin and glutenin, which together form gluten. This, of course, does not mean that sourdough bread does not contain gluten at all, but in such a fermented form, it is better for the body and easier to digest.

Useful compounds for the body

In the fermentation process and also during baking, compounds useful for the body are formed: antioxidants, peptides (lunasin, which acts against cancer cells) and various anti-allergenic substances.

Lower glycaemic index

We are familiar with the claim 'bread is fattening', which is why bread is generally avoided by people with a tendency to be overweight. The fact that white bread made with ordinary baker's yeast leads to weight gain is true. However, sourdough products have a lower glycaemic index due to organic acids that react with heat and consequently reduce starch availability. This index is lower for wholemeal bread types and bread made with sprouted grain flour. Sourdough bread is therefore more filling, and instead of two or three slices, one is often enough. However, due to its excellent taste, it is difficult to stop after just one slice!

Bread stays fresh longer

The acetic acid produced by lactic acid bacteria ensures that sourdough products stay fresh and can be kept for longer, do not crumble and age better. Sourdough bread is still good after a few days, especially rye bread, which gains flavour with time. These naturally occurring acids also prevent mould and fuzzy growths on bread.

A softer crumb

Sourdough gives the crumb a more uniform and compact structure, which is preserved for several days after baking; it is also softer, thanks to lactic acid bacteria.

Better taste

Lactic acid bacteria, and to a lesser extent wild yeast, provide a rich, savoury taste and aroma. During the fermentation process, various aromatic compounds are produced that make sourdough products more palatable.

Better use of nutrients and minerals

Cereals contain naturally occurring phytic acid, which prevents the body from absorbing important minerals such as calcium, magnesium, zinc and iron. By using a sourdough starter and prolonged fermentation, this acidity is neutralised so our bodies can use the minerals present in the flour. Rye flour and wholemeal flour contain the most phytic acid.

No time limit

One advantage of baking with sourdough is that you don't need to stand by the dough while it's proving as you do with commercial yeast due to its fast reaction. This gives you plenty of time to choose the right time for baking and all the other preparation steps, because wild yeast and lactic acid bacteria have a slow metabolism, so the dough rises slowly. While the microorganisms are active, you can do your household chores, go to work, run errands, sleep...

LET'S MAKE AND PREPARE THE STARTER

Good ingredients make for a good sourdough starter and by extension a good bread. When preparing the starter and the bread itself, I make sure that the ingredients I use are locally sourced and organic if possible. That's why I buy most of the flour I use from a cooperative of local produce suppliers and millers that grow and process their own grain.

Initially, the starter will be a bit sensitive, so I recommend using stone-ground flour from a mill and chlorine-free water (filtered or allowed to stand overnight) as chlorine kills yeast and bacteria. Rye flour works more quickly because of its higher mineral content as well as having more microorganisms, but wholemeal wheat flour is also suitable. Use a clean glass jar with a lid so you can observe what's going on in it. The volume should be neither too much nor too little: 360–400 millilitres will be sufficient. Since pesticides and fungicides can also be present in flour, it is better to prepare the starter with organic flour, as fungicides are intended to prevent fungal activity, i.e. yeast – and it is precisely this you want to stimulate.

This is my method and I am very satisfied with it, because it allows me to prepare the starter very quickly. But there are other methods. Some add fresh fruit juice (pineapple juice) to the flour-water mixture, others add strained fruit, and some add kefir, fermented milk or honey. None of these additional ingredients are necessary as they attract other lactic acid bacteria and yeasts not present in the flour. It is possible to succeed with flour from the supermarket, but it is likely to take longer. Don't be discouraged. Wait patiently for life to awaken in this wet mixture and the starter to start bubbling! If you're not comfortable with accurate weighing, prepare a denser mixture with flour (2 heaped teaspoons flour = about 20 g) and water (2 teaspoons water = 10 g), to which you will add more flour and water each day to feed the reproducing microorganisms.

Accessories: clean glass jar with a lid (up to 400 ml), teaspoon, kitchen scales

Ingredients: flour, water, time and patience

Day 1
In a glass jar, mix 20 g of rye flour (the most active) with 20 g of water, partially cover the jar with the lid and leave it in the kitchen or another warm place. In winter you can use slightly warmer water (e.g. 35°C/95°F) and wrap the glass in a towel. Do not leave it on or near a heater, as too high a temperature will affect the development of wild yeast and they could die. Stir lightly twice a day.

Day 2
Add another 20 g of rye flour and 20 g of water to the jar and mix well. Stir lightly twice a day.

Day 3
Add 30 g of rye flour and 30 g of water. You should be able to see the first signs of activity in the jar. The mixture should increase in volume slightly and smell sour. Mix lightly twice a day.

Day 4
Take half of the mixture and use it to make pancakes, for example. Feed the remaining 'mother starter' for three days following the same method as for the third day (to strengthen it and multiply the amount of yeasts and lactic acid bacteria). Mix lightly twice a day.

Day 5
Add 30 g of rye flour and 30 g of water again. Mix lightly twice a day.

Day 6
Add 30 g of rye flour and 30 g of water again. Mix lightly twice a day.

You need to perform this procedure only once, then you can gradually start feeding the mother starter with another type of flour if you don't want to use rye or wholemeal flour (which reacts faster because of their higher nutrient content). You could say that yeasts and lactic acid bacteria are having a party, due to the abundance of nutrients in these two types of flour. If, over these six days, the mixture doubles in less than 24 hours, you can slow it down by refrigerating it until it's next feeding or you can feed early. If the mixture rises

FIRST AID
If the mixture no longer develops after feeding and has a strong acidic smell, remove 5 g of the mixture, put it into a fresh jar. Add 15 g of water and 20 g of flour. Repeat the process if necessary. The mixture should become thick after adding water. Depending on the type of flour you use, the mixture should be neither too fine nor runny.

and falls steadily after the fourth or fifth day, it is ready to use for baking. Bear in mind, however, that at first the starter won't be so strong, so don't get disheartened if you have a flat loaf or two. The older the starter becomes, the more predictable it will be and the better it will be at raising the dough.

By rising and falling, I mean the change in the height of the starter that occurs as the microorganisms digest the flour — in doing so they release carbon dioxide, which results in the mixture increasing as it becomes full of bubbles. However, the mixture collapses if the microorganisms run out of food. You will easily notice this change in height if, after a feeding, you clean the sides of the jar with a spoon and put an elastic band around the jar at the mixture's height. A healthy starter has a pleasant smell of milk with a slight note of lactic acid. If it has an odour of vinegar, it means that the fermentation has gone a little out of control and the starter has turned. But, don't worry, there's a solution for this problem: see page 254 for the chapter 'Starter SOS'!

WHAT'S NEXT?

First of all, I advise you to give your mother starter a name, as this will make it easier to care for it: my 'Rudl' and I are inseparable. To care for your starter, feed it at least once 6–12 hours before each baking. When feeding the starter – i.e. by adding fresh flour and water – take care that it does not become too acidic, as flour is a new food for the existing lactic acid bacteria and wild yeasts. It will make them stronger and allow them to multiply, so that the dough can rise.

The mother starter can be fed with a proportion of 50 g of flour (100 per cent) and 40 g of water (80 per cent). I personally use a mixture of stone-ground organic white wheat flour (50 per cent) and wholemeal wheat flour (50 per cent), so that the starter doesn't work too quickly and I have more room to manoeuvre. For rye flour and wholemeal flour, the ratio of flour to water should be 1:1, because these flours absorb more water. Despite the large proportion of water, a rye starter will not be runny, but it should be frothy by the time you wish to use it.

When the starter is not in use, store it in a refrigerator. Feed it beforehand and reduce the amount of water (by 10–20 per cent) for a thicker mixture. The more time that passes since the last feeding, the weaker the starter will be. If you bake regularly (e.g. once a week), you only need to feed the starter 6–12 hours before baking and leave it at room temperature to encourage the microorganisms to feed. I personally keep 30-40 g of mother starter in my fridge. It is better to have a little less than too much. Smaller quantities are easier to handle.

The starter is ready to use when it rises and falls steadily in a predictable and continuous cycle. It is best to use when it has risen and the surface is no longer bulking but is sinking slightly. This applies to a mother starter in which less water is used, such as up to 80 per cent water, so it looks more like a dough.

For a wheat or spelt starter using a higher water content (100 per cent), in addition to doubling in volume in the glass jar, you can check whether the sourdough is sufficiently active by placing a tablespoon of the starter into water: if it floats, you can use it for the leaven. If the starter sinks, it has run out of food (flour); to revive it simply feed it again and use it when it rises. Do the first aid step on the previous page.

Day 4

Day 5

Day 6

PREPARING THE LEAVEN

The leaven itself is an intermediate step between the starter and the dough. For sourdough, you must use an active starter – 'Rudl', or whatever you wish to call it – and mix it with a larger quantity of flour and water. The more starter you add, the faster the leaven will be ready. This intermediate step with leaven has two purposes: the first is to check how well the starter is working, and the second is to combine it with the flour that will be used to make the bread. The amount of leaven used depends on how fast you want the dough to rise. The more you use, the faster the dough will rise. I personally use 10–30 per cent of leaven, based on the amount of flour in the main dough. If I have 1 kg of flour, I will either prepare 100 to 300 g of leaven, or use as much as 100 to 300 g of the nourished and active 'Rudl' starter.

For example:

Take 10 g of starter (e.g. rye), add 50 g of wheat flour and 40 g of water, or make a dense mixture similar to that of an American-style pancake, or even denser. Then, leave this mixture covered until it at least doubles, rises, and forms bubbles. Use this leaven together with salt after the main dough has sat for a while or undergone autolysis.

I often skip this step, personally, but this is because my starter ('Rudl') is made from a mixture of the two wheat flours in a ratio that I most often use. Also, my jar is large enough (360 ml) to hold the ingredients (about 120 g) that I use in the main dough. In addition, it is possible to take a small amount of starter and use it to produce a larger amount of starter, which will make it easier to raise the dough in a relatively short time.

When I take a given amount for the leaven, I leave very little starter in the jar – usually 5–10 g (a small spoonful) – and then add 20 g of flour (4 teaspoons) and 15 g of water (1 tablespoon) to form a denser mixture, and then I leave it at room temperature for about an hour before putting it into the fridge. However, I make the intermediate leaven when baking with spelt or rye flour. If your starter is of white plain wheat flour or strong flour, and you are planning to feed it before baking so that the result will be risen and bubbly, you can freely use it instead of the leaven; otherwise, follow the intermediate steps when preparing the recipes in this book.

SWEET STIFF STARTER

I first stumbled on the preparation of a sweet starter in 2016 in Belgium when Stefan Cappele introduced it at The Quest for Sourdough event, which I will talk about in the chapter 'The World's First Sourdough Library'. I have been using this starter ever since. It is suitable for baking sweet delicacies such as brioche, croissants, doughnuts, sweet plaits, cakes, etc. It is made from the mother starter (20 per cent), strong white flour, small amounts of water (40-45 per cent) and sugar (25 per cent). Knead to obtain a firm dough, wait for it to at least triple in size, then use in the dough. By adding sugar to the starter, the wild yeasts becomes more active and reproductive, helping the heavier dough to rise more easily.

GLUTEN-FREE STARTER AND GLUTEN-FREE BREAD

Gluten-free flours do not contain gluten. These include buckwheat, maize, millet, teff, quinoa and others. Even with gluten-free flour, it's possible to make delicious, soft bread. Once again, lactic acid bacteria and wild yeast raises the dough during fermentation. Gluten-free starters are prepared similarly to gluten ones: mix 1 part of flour (100 per cent) and 1.2 parts of water (120 per cent) as gluten-free flour absorbs a lot of water. The flour-water mixture must be more runny. Gluten-free starters become active faster and you can use it to make bread after two or three days. As a binder, we add psyllium seeds, from 5–6 per cent by weight of flour. There is no need to scald the flour when preparing 100 per cent gluten-free bread.

WILD YEAST WATER

Because wild yeasts and lactic acid bacteria are present everywhere, so-called wild yeast water can be prepared from fruits, vegetables, plants and flowers. In 2016 my friend Midori Asano published on Perfect Sourdough's Facebook group a guide for preparing this wild yeast water, which is typical of East Asian dough preparation. Guy Frenkel also recommends the same method. Before you begin, make sure that the ingredients you want to ferment are edible and capable of fermentation. Then, according to size, cut into pieces, place it in a large clear wide-mouthed jar, and fill up to three quarters with water (preferably left to stand or filtered).

It is not necessary to add sugar for fruits and vegetables. For flowers or plants add 10–30 per cent sugar based on the total weight of water and plants (preferably soft brown sugar or honey). Sugar is a natural food for yeasts and bacteria. Put the lid on the jar and shake well, then leave to rest in a warm place. Shake and vent off the gas twice daily. After a few days (2–6), the contents will start to bubble, and when you vent the jar foam and bubbles will appear. You can then sieve and use wild yeast water to prepare the starter. Mix equal parts of water and flour, wait for the mixture to rise and then use it as a leaven for the main dough.

You can store the rest of the water in the refrigerator, adding some sugar so that the wild yeasts will have enough food. In wild yeast water, there is significantly more yeast than lactic acid bacteria, and the dough ferments faster and does not acidify as quickly. The lower number of lactic acid bacteria also results

in less lactic and acetic acid, which contributes to a less pronounced, better taste. The composition, nutritional value and efficiency of wild yeast water are currently being researched.

THE WORLD'S FIRST SOURDOUGH LIBRARY

When I was invited to Belgium in September 2016 to visit the world's first sourdough library, I admit that I had no idea what to expect. I was very surprised to have been selected, even though I was very active at the time on the Facebook group Perfect Sourdough, which is managed by Teresa L. from the United States. At this event we got to know each other better and became friends. So I accepted the invitation and the challenge and flew off to new adventures. I asked myself all sorts of questions: why create such a library, what is being done, what is its purpose, why was I invited, what are the objectives, etc.?

Puratos, one of the largest manufacturers of bakery, confectionery, ice cream and gastronomy ingredients, started collecting the first samples of sourdough in 1989. In 2013, the company opened the world's first not-for-profit sourdough library with 43 samples, the result of a long-standing research programme in collaboration with Professor Marco Gobbetti of the University of Bari. The library currently contains 128 sourdough samples from 24 countries, namely Italy, Austria, France, Germany, the Netherlands, Japan, Spain, China, Mexico, Hungary, Greece, Denmark, the United States, Great Britain, Australia, Brazil, Switzerland, Peru, Portugal, Singapore, Turkey, Canada and Slovenia.

These samples, made available to the library by their owners, most often traditional bakeries, are preserved in jars under specific and controlled conditions. As a result, you can find in the library the starter used for traditional types of bread, such as the bread from the Altamura region, the starter from Mexico used to make the traditional Mexican *birote* bread, the starter from San Francisco and many others. In October 2019, my 'Rudl' also took his place in the library by becoming the first Slovenian starter. All these starters are entrusted to the librarian Karl de Smedt, who devotes himself to his task with great enthusiasm and passion.

At the time of being added to the library, each sample is thoroughly analysed to determine precisely the strains of lactic acid bacteria and wild yeasts present in the sourdough, so that a complete documentation of the composition of each sourdough sample is available.

All samples and their composition can also be consulted in the Internet library at the following address www.puratossourdoughlibrary.com. So far, more than 1,100 different microorganisms have been found in these samples.

The aim of the library is to preserve as many as possible sourdough types for future generations, to promote biodiversity and to disseminate knowledge about sourdough baking. In addition, the owners of the starters always have a secure supply in case something happens to their mother starter.

The library itself is a non-profit initiative by Puratos, contributing to the wonderful world of natural fermentation and fermentation technology. It also provides a better understanding of all aspects of sourdough preparation and encourages in-depth research to enable the company to meet the needs of its customers.

The starter samples kept by the library remain the property of their donors and are not reproduced or sold by Puratos. Owners only have to provide 25 kg of flour per year. This flour is then used in the library to feed the starter. This operation takes place every two months for four days, under controlled conditions to avoid contamination by local microorganisms. The samples are then returned to the refrigerator, where they rest at a temperature of 2–4°C/35–39°F until the next time.

In September 2016, in addition to this physical collection, the Sourdough Library project was presented on the internet. Everyone can register their starter, describe it, and add a photograph and recipe for its preparation. If you visit the www.questforsourdough.com, you'll find so many different starters. More than 2,000 are already registered there, including my Rudl. Many personalities from the world of sourdough making were invited to participate in this project, including simple amateurs, all sharing the same enthusiasm for this method of preparation.

The reflection that concluded this event also touched me greatly: the future of bread lies in its past. I can only agree with that. And so I hope that this book will also contribute to the dissemination of the use of sourdough.

THE ONLINE LIBRARY
QUEST FOR SOURDOUGH

In September 2016, Puratos completed its physical collection of sourdough with an online version of its library. Within the framework of this project, many personalities from the world of sourdough making were invited to Belgium by the librarian Karl de Smedt. Guests ranged from amateur bakers to big names from baking schools, all sharing the same enthusiasm for this method of preparation. It was on this occasion that professional bakers were brought together for the first time: Yohant Ferrant, William Woo, Beesham Soogrim, Vanessa Kimbell, Manfred Enoksson, Olivier Penet, Patrick Willaert, but also amateurs: Teresa, already mentioned before, Guy Frenkel, Ralph Nieboer, Carol Lee, Ineke Berentschot, Jarkko Laine and myself. This family of 14 sourdough bakers from all over the world was joined by the two sourdough experts Stefan Cappelle and Stéphane van Cauwenbergh, as well as the technical advisor Morgan Clementson.

Although at first in doubt, I accepted Karl's invitation and flew to Brussels for the first time with Rudl. From the airport, I took a taxi to Saint-Vith, a small town near the German border. There, next to the Puratos factory, stands the imposing building of the Center for Bread Flavour. It houses the Sourdough Library. The event was perfectly prepared, all the details planned and carefully studied. During these three days spent in Saint-Vith, I was able to forget all my doubts and enjoy spending time with the other participants. Yes, we can talk about sourdough, kneading the dough, shaping and baking for hours on end. We also visited the Sourdough Library and toured the nearby Puratos manufacturing plant. From being strangers to each other, in three days we became true friends, bound together by love, passion and dedication to the preparation of sourdough. We were all looking forward to the last day, to be told the purpose of the invitation. And, indeed, Karl presented us with a video presentation of The Quest for Sourdough, and we were privileged to be the first to discover this project. We have become ambassadors of the Sourdough Library. Back home, it took me several days to figure out what had just happened and what was waiting for me next.

This experience in Belgium completely changed my view of sourdough. New horizons opened up for me. I had started to explore the subject beforehand, but later I created my Instagram profile (sourdough_mania), and with it my media recognition was immediate, first abroad and then in Slovenia.

Each starter is particular, distinctive. Flavour, ingredients and texture: sourdough is influenced by so many different factors! I invite you to discover why your starters are unique. Register them online at: www.questforsourdough.com. Describe them, take photographs, add your preparation tips and share them with sourdough enthusiasts around the world. You can also browse and search for the different types of starter already online.

your firstborn

Bread is the staple food without which it would be difficult to imagine life on a daily basis – and the oldest method of raising it is sourdough. Before the discovery of this process, all breads were flat.

But what does it take to make a certain success of this bread? It's very simple! Just flour, water and salt, a little time and a lot of love and patience. Of course, you can also add other ingredients to the bread dough, such as sesame, nuts, olives or cheese. As you will see later, sourdough use is by no means limited to bread. In the second part of this book, you will find recipes for sweet sourdough delights. And you will also find some recipes for using sourdough in cooking.

FLOUR

When you start baking, I recommend you use wheat flour, the simplest being to use white plain wheat flour (type 550) and strong flour (type 812). Do not mix too many types of flour at once, possibly two at most, and do not add more than 30 per cent gluten-free flour that you have previously scald (e.g. buckwheat or maize flour). Wholemeal bread will be just as good and will have a soft crumb if you use with half a white plain wheat or strong flour.

WATER

The water should be at room temperature and, if possible, left to stand or filtered. If you want to slow down the starter activity, use very cold water, otherwise warm it up a little to 35°C/95°F. But take care, as when water is too hot, the whole process proceeds too quickly – and time is an important ingredient in the preparation of sourdough. There is no need for haste.

SALT

Salt inhibits the activity of microorganisms, so it should be added after autolysis. It also strengthens the gluten. You can adjust the amount of salt to your taste. I use Slovenian coarse salt, which I grind at home in my food processor.

In addition to flour, water and salt, which are the main components of the dough, you can add the following ingredients to refine and enrich your bakes:

MILK

The milk softens the bakes, giving them regular holes and a nice brown crust. The milk indicated in the recipes is full-fat milk. If you use fresh milk, it should be boiled and allowed to cool.

FATS

The presence of fat in the dough extends its shelf life and gives a softer crumb. As they inhibit gluten development, they are added after autolysis, when the gluten mesh has already developed and strengthened. The fats must be at room temperature, and in the case of butter, it must not be melted. If you add oil to recipes, reduce the amount of water by the amount of oil used.

EGGS

I use eggs with milk, salt, and sometimes a little cream to glaze before baking, as they make the crust nicely brown. Also, the crumb becomes even and softer.

SUGAR

A small amount of sugar (up to 5 per cent) encourages yeast and bacteria activity, but a larger amount slows it down. When making sweet dough, use the sweet starter – see the recipe on page 63. I use unrefined soft brown sugar for recipes myself in smaller amounts. Follow the recipe instructions at first, then adjust the quantity to your taste when you're ready to experiment.

ADDITIONS (seeds, fruits, nuts, flakes, wholegrains, etc.)

You can add seeds, pieces of fruit and nuts, up to 10–20 per cent by weight of flour, to bread or roll recipes. Soak them overnight before use; you can also add a teaspoon of sourdough. Subtract the amount of water in which you soak these additions from the amount of water in the recipe. If the dough is too dry, you can still add water later. You can also boil wholegrain cereals in twice the amount of water and allow them to swell. If these additions are larger, add them after the third round of stretch and folds, and in the case of smaller ones (e.g. sesame seeds) you can add them after the first rising. You can also roast seeds and nuts before soaking.

TIME

Remember, time is an important factor in sourdough baking, so don't rush. Wait for the wild yeasts and lactic acid bacteria to do their job. The taste and aromas develop slowly during the first rise, which also serves to strengthen the dough. Therefore, it is possible to bulk prove the dough in the refrigerator, where the dough will slowly strengthen and develop. You can also put the shaped dough in the refrigerator for the final prove.

USEFUL EQUIPMENT

Electronic scales – At the beginning, it is best to weigh the ingredients and be meticulous, so scales with an accuracy of 1 g are most suitable. Later on, when you have acquired a sense of quantity, you will be able to do without the scales when making bread.

One or more containers with a lid of at least 2 litres capacity – You will use them to mix the dough and let it rise, so they must be big enough. Glass containers make it easier to see what's going on in the dough. The lid prevents the top layer of dough from drying out. If the container does not have a lid, you can also use a bag, a damp cloth or a shower cap, which are also suitable for covering a proving basket.

Wooden spoon or spatula – A wooden spoon or spatula will be used to mix all the ingredients at first and will be useful for certain types of dough that contain a lot of rye flour.

Spoon – Using the spoon handle is the easiest way to stir your starter in a jar.

Metal or plastic bench knife – This dough knife will easily divide dough into smaller pieces, and you can also use it to shape the dough and transfer it to a proving basket.

Rounded plastic scraper – Very handy when you want to scrape all the dough out of the container, it can also be used to stretch and fold a wet dough.

Baking tray or steel plate, terracotta, enamel or cast-iron casserole with a lid – You can use any of these utensils. Everything must be preheated at the same time as the oven for at least 45 minutes. To obtain the effect of a bread oven, it is better to use a casserole. If you don't have a casserole, you can also flip a high rimmed tin over the bread.

Fine sieve – Sifting aerates the flour, allows more oxygen to enter and removes lumps. It also makes it easier to detect hidden visitors.

Large tea strainer – A great help if you want to dust flour on the work surface, the cloth in the proving basket or the surface of the dough before scoring it.

Proving basket (*Banneton*) – Used to prepare the dough, as it supports it so that the dough does not collapse and retains its shape. There are baskets of various sizes for different quantities and shapes of dough. The materials are also diverse: they can be natural (reed, rattan, wood pulp) or artificial (plastic). If you don't have one, you can improvise and use a plastic strainer, a bread basket with a high rim, or an ordinary container in which to place a linen or cotton cloth. The size of the container must be adapted to the amount of dough: if it is too small, the dough will lose its grip and spill out; if it is too large, the dough is not held sufficiently during rising and will run out as it rises.

Linen or cotton cloth for rising – You can place a cloth in the proving basket and moisten it to prevent the dough sticking to the basket. You can also use a larger cloth as a support for baguettes by folding it.

Pizza or bread shovel – This makes it easier to push the dough into the oven.

Mould or baking form – For certain types of bread or other bakes that contain more liquid or are made from enriched dough. (Sizes are indicated within the respective recipes).

High rimmed tin – Place it in the bottom of the oven and add boiling water to produce steam if you don't have a lid on the casserole or if you are cooking large amounts at a time.

Baking paper – A practical accessory when you want to put the dough in an oven or casserole. Reusable baking paper is available.

Food wrap, shower cap – To cover the dough and prevent it drying out; reusable. You can also make a coated cloth yourself and use it to cover the dough, as suggested by Duši, a participant at a workshop.

Oven gloves – To protect hands from burns. You can also use thick cloths.

Food processor – It is not absolutely essential, but it is practical for enriched doughs (brioche, fritters, rolls, etc.) in which butter or oil is added.

And let's not forget, you'll also need an **oven.**

STEP-BY-STEP DOUGH PREPARATION

In this chapter, we will look at all the steps involved in making bread dough, using the recipe example called 'Bread in a Flash' (page 152). Unless otherwise specified, you can use the same process for all other recipes. I will explain to you, with the help of pictures, what the different steps are and why they are necessary.

This strong flour-based bread is prepared according to a specific principle, which consists of using one part of active ingredients for every two parts of water and three parts of flour. Weigh your mother starter, which must be active and bubbly. This means that you fed it 6–12 hours before using it and waited until the quantity had at least doubled. Then multiply its weight by two to get the amount of water and by three to calculate the amount of flour.

You can also use a mixture of other types of flour, with plain flour and strong flour being the most suitable. For spelt flour, reduce the amount of water by 10 per cent, for rye and wholemeal flour, add a little more water: 5–10 per cent. Don't forget that because of the greater quantity of these flours, the bread will have a denser crumb, smaller holes and will therefore be more compact. Due to the greater amount of starter in the recipe, it will also rise more quickly.

PREPARING AND WEIGHING INGREDIENTS

Weigh and prepare all the necessary ingredients, i.e. flour, water, starter and salt. At the beginning, it is best to weigh the quantities. Once you master the processes and the preparation, this will no longer be necessary, at least not for bread. I also recommend repeating a recipe several times. As far as I am concerned, I sift the flour before the mixing so that it is aerated and softer.

100 g active starter (33%)
200 g water (66%)
300 g strong white bread (type 812) flour (100%)
6 g salt (2%)

PREMIXING AND AUTOLYSIS

At first, mix only the flour and water in a container so that the mixture is not dry and to obtain a smooth mixture. Mix just until all the flour is well soaked with water, without kneading it. Leave this dough to rest for at least 20 minutes, then you can shape and knead it more easily.

This process is called autolysis, meaning the degradation of cells with their own enzymes. The term and the technique were first used by Frenchman Raymond Calvel. Adding water to the flour activates the enzymes it contains. The two most important enzymes are amylase, which breaks down compound sugars or carbohydrates (starch) into simple sugars, which are then used to feed yeast, and protease, which breaks down proteins (including gluten).

Gluten consists of two proteins, gliadin and glutenin, which combine and swell on contact with water to form gluten chains, which in turn form a network or mesh. Since yeast produces carbon dioxide in addition to ethanol during fermentation, this carbon dioxide remains in the glutinous mesh. This allows the dough to rise and the bread to keep its shape later, with a nice crumb, i.e. with regular holes. But even gluten compounds are not infinitely elastic. If the enzymes are too active, these compounds begin to dissolve and the dough collapses or is reduced to a large piece of leaven. So you have to find the right balance, the maximum rising point of the dough, but you will know more about this in the piece on rising (page 83).

Autolysis is not essential, but it does make the dough more beautiful and easier to shape. It can last from 20 minutes to 2 hours or more if you put the dough in the refrigerator immediately after autolysis. Flours with the highest protein content (the best gluten) tolerate longer autolysis. At the end of this step, you will notice that the dough is smoother, softer and more relaxed. While resting, the dough works for you and you can devote yourself to other tasks.

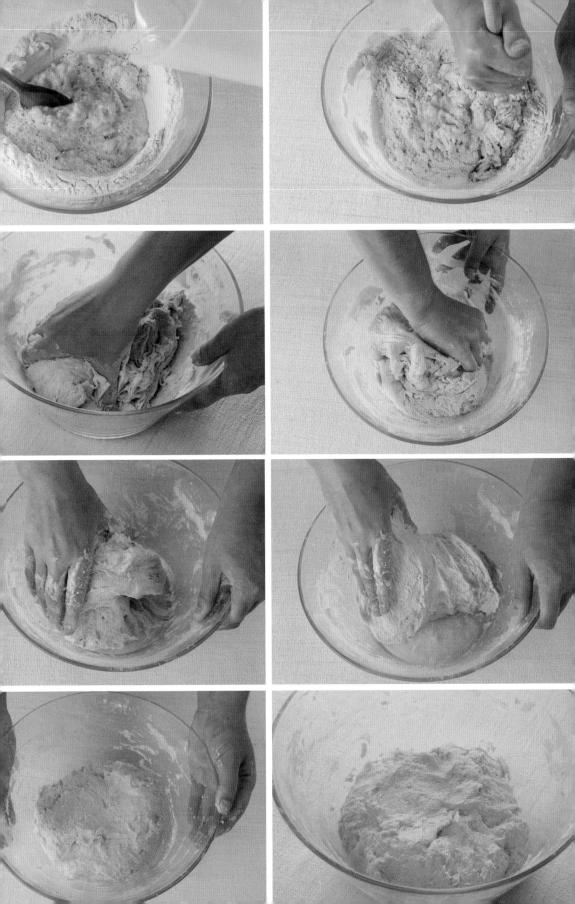

FIRST RISE

After the autolysis of the dough, add the starter, which will allow the dough to rise, and incorporate the salt. Knead everything well so that all the ingredients are incorporated and form a dough. For my part, I spread the starter on the surface of the dough before sprinkling the salt evenly. Notice how the salt contracts and strengthens the gluten bonds.

Just touch the dough containing salt with your fingers to feel this effect! It also acts as a preservative, adds flavour to bread, colours the crust and slows down the activity of microorganisms, i.e. the bacteria and wild yeasts.

After this kneading, let the dough rest, covered, in the container so that it ferments and rises. It must double in volume until it is light and airy before you shape it. During the rising phase in the container (bulk fermentation), you can also put the dough in the refrigerator, where it will mature and develop a stronger taste. I often do that. If the dough is placed in the refrigerator, you should check that it has at least doubled in volume since the addition of the starter before beginning the preshaping. If it has not risen sufficiently, leave it to rest at room temperature for a while. During rising, the dough (the gluten strands) becomes stronger, and the taste and structure are strengthened.

TIP

If you don't have time, you can mix all the ingredients (i.e. flour, water, starter and salt) and knead well. Leave the dough to rise at room temperature until it has almost doubled in volume. Shape it and put it into a proving basket or mould. Leave it to rise again and put it into the oven. This is an alternative way, but every step has its purpose. In fact, I myself recommend a longer fermentation of more than 15 hours. Meanwhile, the dough should be kept in the refrigerator, otherwise it will rise too much and begin to collapse.

KNEADING

After adding the salt, incorporate the salt and starter into the dough with your fingertips. As for me, I press and turn several times with my whole hand (like a screw) and while pressing, I make sure that the salt and starter blend well into the dough. When pressing, I take care not to tear the dough (the gluten strands) and only go as far as necessary to obtain a smooth dough. Although it may seem at first glance that the dough does not completely absorb the starter and salt, don't worry – all the ingredients will soon combine.

Leave the dough to rest for 10 minutes to allow the gluten to relax a little. Always cover the container to prevent the formation of a crust (crusting) on the surface of the dough. After 10 minutes, start the premix.

This step is not absolutely essential. You've probably already made bread without kneading. But the purpose of kneading is to strengthen the gluten strands, which can then retain the amount of carbon dioxide that the wild yeast produces during fermentation. The more gluten you develop, the more the bread will gain in volume. You can also use a food processor, but in this case you must be careful not to over-knead the dough. In the worst case, water may leak out.

There are different kneading methods. It's up to you to find the one that suits you best. Here are some of the ones I use most often. I usually knead two or three times, every 2–3 minutes. You can visualise the evolution of gluten before and after kneading with the window pane test: stretch the dough and pay attention to its structure. After kneading, it will be much more regular and beautiful. If you use wholemeal flour, the bran somewhat hinders the development of a good structure.

As the gluten strands contract during kneading, the dough should rest for at least 10–15 minutes after each kneading step, so that it can relax again. If you're not comfortable kneading in the bowl, you can knead on the work surface. In any case, your contact with the dough should be as short and as quick as possible. This short and quick contact also applies to all subsequent steps. Before kneading, you can moisten your hands slightly, but not too much, otherwise you will add too much water to the dough.

NORMAL KNEADING OF DOUGH

Grasp the dough in your hands, press it down and knead it in the way that suits you best.

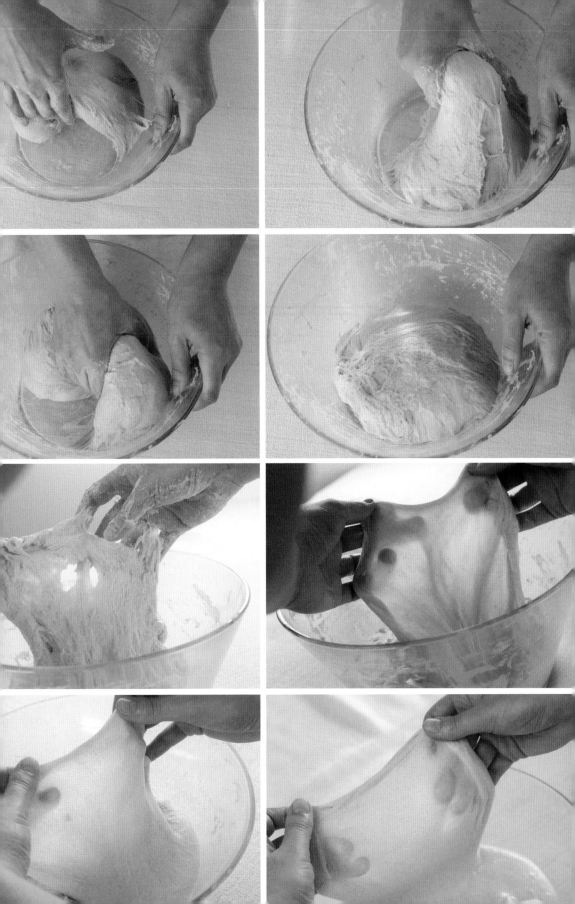

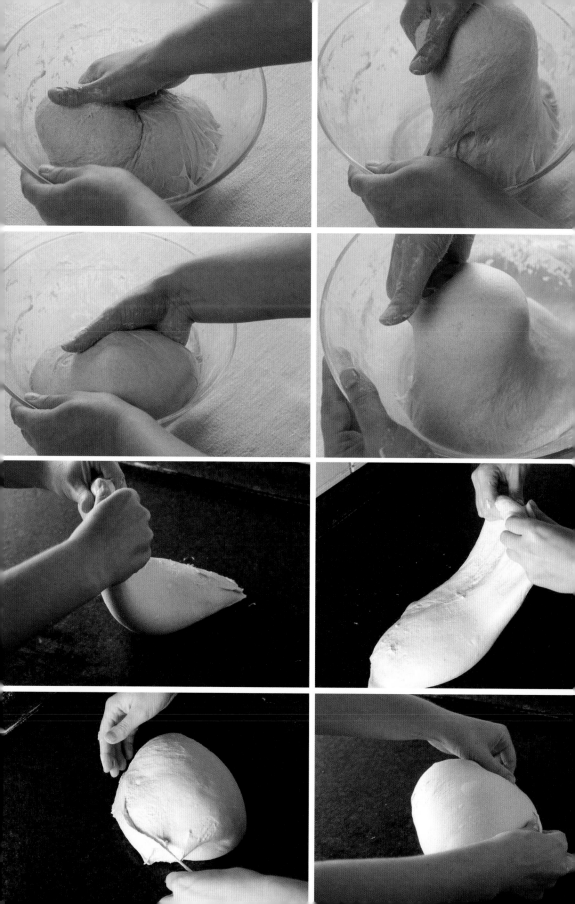

SCOOP AND STRETCH

It's the technique I use most often. You probably remember how our grandmothers used to whip the dough with a wooden spoon – the kneading method is similar. With this scoop and stretch technique, you grasp the dough with the whole palm of your hand and your fingers closed under the dough, lift it up as quickly as possible and stretch it upwards to strengthen the gluten.

SLAP AND FOLD ON THE WORK TOP

This is a good technique for a dough containing more water. Moisten the work surface a little and take the dough out of the container with a rounded scraper. Grasp the dough with both hands on one side, lift it vertically and stretch it. Slap the dough on the surface and fold it over (slap and fold). Repeat this several times. With each press on the work surface, the dough becomes smoother and softer. You can repeat the process until the gluten contracts and no further bending is possible.

STRETCH AND FOLD

This method allows the gluten to be strengthened during the rising in the bowl. It is also to distribute the food available to wild yeasts and lactic acid bacteria, to balance the temperature of the dough and to add air to the dough.

Within 2 hours after the last kneading, stretch and fold once every 20–30 minutes, four times in total. The last time, handle the dough more gently, since it already contains some carbon dioxide. Grasp one end of the bowl, with your hand under the edge of the dough and grasp it with folded fingers. Pull the dough up and towards you so that it does not tear and fold it over. Repeat this operation all around the bowl.

For my part, I like to ball the dough after each pass, so that it has a nice surface.

I do this by pushing the palm of my hand at an angle under the dough and applying pressure in one direction while pushing the bowl in the opposite direction with my other hand.

TIP

If the dough, and the gluten in particular, is not yet sufficiently developed, you can stretch and fold more often. If you don't have the time, simply skip the stretching and folding step.

DOUGH BEFORE RISING

APPROPRIATELY RISEN DOUGH FOR PRESHAPING

PRESHAPING

Preforming or preshaping is used to strengthen the gluten strands, and also gives the boule or batard its subsequent shape, making the final shaping easier. This process also creates tension on the surface of the dough so that the dough can support its own weight during baking. When the volume of the dough has approximately doubled, it has risen sufficiently and can be preshaped. If you now place it on a flat surface, its edges will be slightly rounded and it hardly distorts any more, as it already contains enough carbon dioxide. At this stage, you can also divide the dough if you wish to obtain several pieces of dough.

Dust the work surface with flour. The amount of flour depends on the moisture content of the dough: if the dough is moist enough, use a little more flour, otherwise use less. Gradually you will have a more precise idea of the amount of flour to use on the work surface. There should not be too much flour, otherwise the dough would not stick and would just slide on the work surface. Before removing the dough from the bowl with a scraper and spreading it out on the work surface, moisten the utensil slightly. This makes it much easier to remove the dough from the bowl, but also to preserve the bubbles. Handle this dough with care if you want even holes. You can remove the larger bubbles by lightly tapping the dough with your hands. When you put the dough under tension, there should be just enough to prevent the surface tearing.

For a round loaf (Fr. *boule*) or a long loaf (Fr. *bâtard*), spread the dough into a square shape, then pull a little on the top half, fold it two thirds of the way and gently press it onto the flap. Then take the left side of the dough, pull it out a little and fold it to the right, always two thirds of the way. Then take the right-hand side and fold it over with a slight pull to the left, again two thirds of the way. Only the lower part is left, pull it out a little and fold it up two thirds of the way. Finally, turn the shaped loaf so that the smooth side faces upwards and the join is facing down. You can also use a dough bench knife for this. Scatter a little flour over the bread and cover it with a cloth.

If the dough is very wet, you can spray water on the work surface before shaping the dough with a bench knife. To put the dough into tension, there must be some adhesion between the dough and the work surface – gently push the bench knife between the dough and the work surface and make a circular motion around the dough.

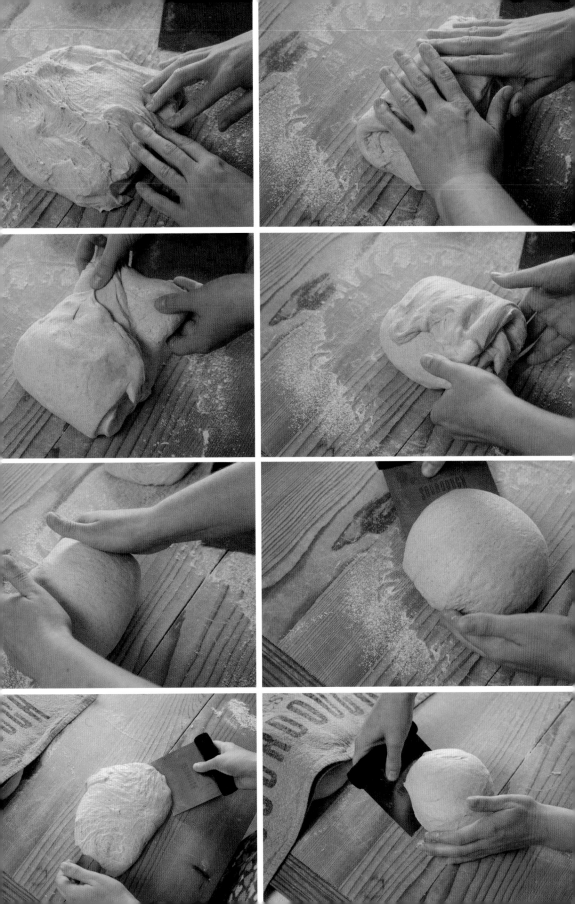

BENCH RESTING

After preshaping, leave the dough to rest on the work surface for at least 15–25 minutes (bench resting). During this time, the gluten will relax, the dough will stretch slightly and the final shaping will be easier. If it spreads out too much, you can preshape it again and leave it to rest on the work surface for a while so that it grows a little more.

FINAL SHAPING

During the final shaping, you have one last opportunity to strengthen the dough and create tension on the surface. Flour the dough a little more before turning it over, top side down on the work surface, using the bench knife. The side that rested on the work surface is now turned upwards and the smooth side is underneath. I will present here the methods I use most often. There are others: it's up to you to find the one that suits you best.

THE FINAL SHAPING OF A BOULE

You can repeat the preshaping steps or you can fold all the corners of the dough inwards with your fingers, holding them in the middle with your thumb. Repeat the process until there is no more dough to be folded inwards. Then turn the bread over again with the bench knife so that the smooth side is at the top and the part where all the edges touch is underneath. With lightly floured hands, you can turn the bread over a few times, pressing with the palms of your hands on the work surface and the lower part of the bread. Repeat this process until a nice tension is created on the surface of the dough – which should not tear. When you turn the dough this way, there should be as little flour as possible or hardly any flour at all on the work surface, otherwise you will not be able to create friction and will only push the dough onto the surface. Wait 2–3 minutes for the bottom of the dough to stick and flour the top.

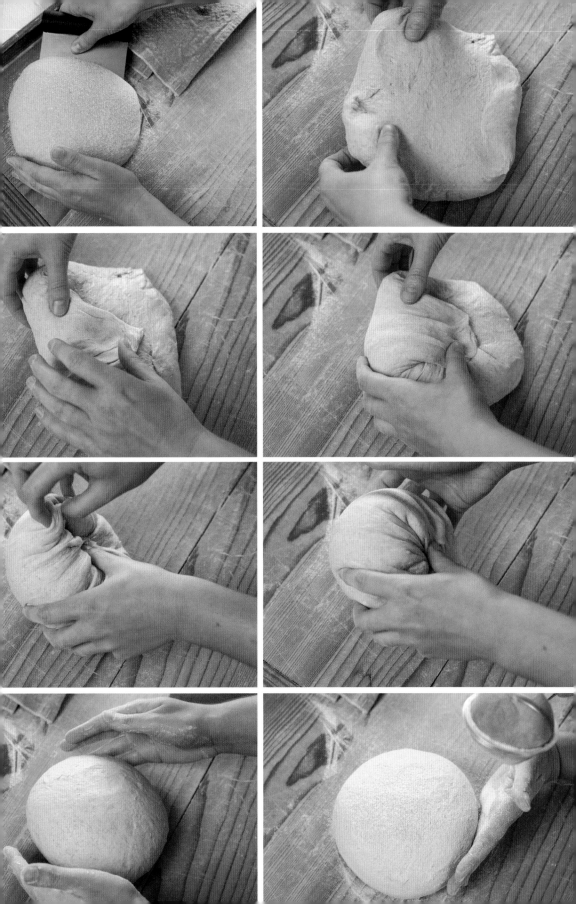

THE FINAL SHAPING OF A BATARD

When you turn the dough on the smooth surface, fold the two corners inwards to form the batard. Then start turning the dough towards you with your fingers, pressing your thumbs on the joins and pulling them away from you a little. In the meantime you can fold the left and right sides of the dough inwards. When you reach the end, press a little more on the joining line. To tension the surface of the dough, you can also use a bench knife on one side and your hand on the other. This shaping method is also suitable for bread that is to be baked in a baking tin, e.g. for the loaf on page 156.

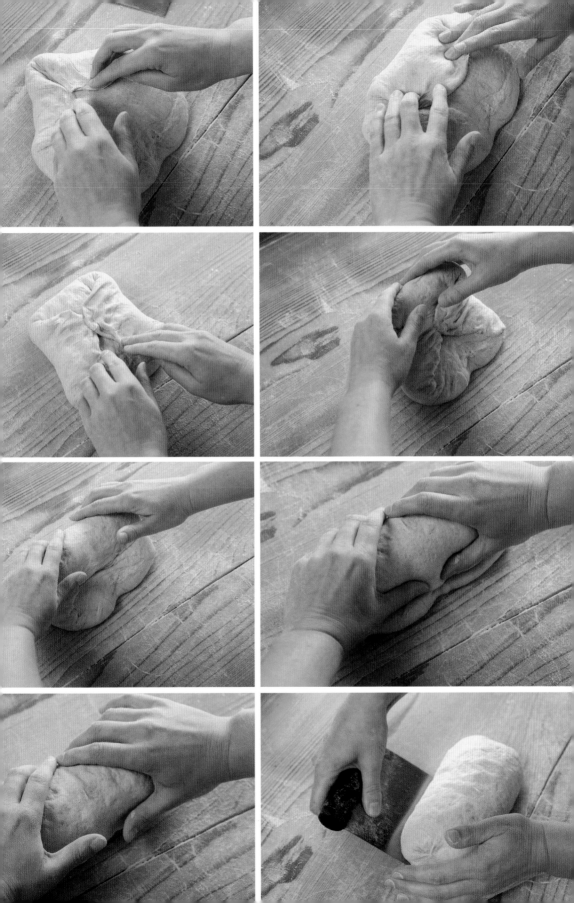

PREPARING A PROVING BASKET

You can use the proving basket (or banneton) with or without linen. If you don't use it, the basket will leave a nice pattern on the surface of the dough. In this case, however, you must first sprinkle it with a little water before flouring it well, as the dough likes to stick to the basket, especially when it contains a lot of liquid. The best flours, the ones that prevent the dough sticking to the basket or cloth, are, in order, rice flour, maize flour and buckwheat flour (all of which are gluten-free and therefore do not form dough when in contact with water), semolina (very useful for pushing a pizza from a shovel or tray into the oven), bran, wholemeal flour and, last but not least, white flour.

If you are using a cloth, place it in the basket in such a way that there are as few folds as possible and that they overlap. Use a linen cloth, as linen has the natural ability to wick away or retain just the right amount of moisture. Then come the cotton cloths or tea towels. You can also buy special liners, which you can then adapt to the basket as best as possible. Whatever you use, flour generously. If there is too much flour, you can always remove the excess with a brush before baking. It is not necessary to wash these cloths after each use, as a thin film forms on them over time, the cloths become starched, which prevents them sticking. From time to time (about two to three times a year), I wash them without a softener.

FINAL RISE

After shaping, place the boule or batard in the floured proving basket. Use the bench knife to push under the dough while supporting it with your other hand. Then lift the dough and place it in the basket so that the smooth side is underneath again. You can also place the dough in the basket in such a way that the other side of the dough, i.e. where you joined the pieces of dough, faces down. The bread will then open at this point during baking and will not need to be scored. This final fermentation is known as the final proving. After 2–3 hours at room temperature, you can put the shaped and covered dough into the proofing basket or in a baking tin and place in the refrigerator, where it will rise slowly.

REMOVING DOUGH FROM THE BASKET

To help remove the dough from the basket, support the dough with one hand and turn the basket with the other. You can also put baking paper on the basket, put a baking tray or shovel over it and then turn the basket over.

After use, shake the excess flour from the basket and dry it so that it does not become mouldy and parasites do not proliferate. If the basket is made of natural materials, you can also put it into the oven at a low temperature after baking the bread (up to a 100°C/212°F) to dry it.

WHEN IS THE DOUGH READY FOR BAKING?

There is no precise answer to this question, as timing is a difficult element to determine. The speed of growth is indeed influenced by different factors: the quantity and age of the starter, the water temperature, the ambient temperature, the quality of the development of the gluten, etc. But rest assured, the more bread you make, the quicker you will know when the right moment has come. When you use a starter, time is your ally. This is because the time it takes for the sourdough to reach maturity is much longer than when you use ordinary yeast.

Some of the tips in this chapter should give you a better understanding on timing. As with all the other steps, you must use all your senses to accompany the dough. Start by observing its rise from the moment you put it in the basket or on the baking tray. Before baking, it should almost double again. If you have done the final proving in the refrigerator, check before baking that the shaped dough has grown sufficiently since the final shaping. If it has not risen sufficiently, leave it to rest at room temperature for a short time.

In addition to observing the volume, the finger test is also a good indicator. Push your finger a good centimetre into the dough. When the dough is just ready to bake, the indentation closes slowly but not completely, and it's time to preheat the oven. In the meantime, you can put the dough in the refrigerator to firm up a little. If the dough has not yet risen sufficiently, the hole will quickly close again, in which case you will have to wait a little longer before baking. If the indentation remains intact, the dough is over fermented. Gluten strands can no longer retain carbon dioxide and have started to degrade. But don't worry, bake the dough anyway. The bread will be good and hearty, although it might not increase in size any more in the oven, and it may collapse or fall apart a bit. Remember this experience for next time. Do not perform this test immediately after the final shaping, as it would not be revealing at that time, nor when you take the shaped and risen dough out of the refrigerator. For a better comparison, test the dough about 30 minutes after placing it in the proving basket or in the baking tin.

Fermentation and rising overlap a little. Fermentation is the umbrella term, with rising being part of the fermentation process or a side effect of the yeast producing carbon dioxide.

FINGER TEST

NOT ENOUGH

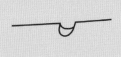

Press a finger 1 cm deep into the dough. If the hole closes quickly and completely, wait a little longer.

READY

The hole is closing slowly and almost completely: it's time to preheat the oven.

TOO MUCH

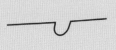

If the hole remains intact, the dough is over fermented. Cook it anyway.

SCORING AND DECORATION

Make an incision in the dough just before putting it in the oven. Scoring is not only for decoration, but also allows the bread to swell well in the oven. A properly leavened dough takes on even more volume and the bread gets bigger. Evenly distributed incisions on the surface contribute to a good distribution of the dough in the oven. These incisions also allow the dough to open exactly where you want it to. If you don't slice it, the dough may open at the weakest point. But if you place it on the tray with the seam facing upwards, the bread will open up exactly there. In this case, there is no need to score.

You can use different ways to score. Professional bakers use a special blade to cut through the dough. You can also use an ordinary razor blade, holding it between your fingers or attaching it to a chopstick or skewer. A scalpel or a very sharp knife can be used to make precise incisions. You can also create original shapes with scissors – flowers, dinosaurs, etc.

When scoring, your movements must be fast and precise; you must not pull on the dough, just cut it. If you lightly flour the surface, the dough will be easier to score. You can also moisten or oil the blade. Refrigerated dough is much easier to score than dough that has risen at room temperature. To get 'ears' or a raised edge in the bread, you must cut it at an angle of 30-45 degrees. If, on the other hand, you want the dough to spread across the width, cut it perpendicular to the surface. If the dough has risen/fermented too much, avoid scoring it, because it could then collapse due to the weakening of the gluten network. With a little practice, you'll find the ideal depth. When the dough has risen well, I score it to a depth of 0.5-1 cm to get ears. Don't forget that the scoring is in a way the baker's signature. It's up to you to find your own.

USING A STENCIL

Another type of decoration is done using stencils. For a contrasting pattern, use flour, cocoa or other coloured powders (e.g. turmeric, ground paprika or seaweed such as spirulina). Place the stencil on the dough and you could also moisten it so that the pattern adheres better. Then dust. Tea strainers are particularly useful for this. Carefully remove the stencil to avoid damaging the pattern. You can also score the dough before putting it in the oven. In this case, do not spray the dough in the oven while baking, as this may damage the pattern. It is best to place a deep tin filled with water at the base of the oven or to bake in a cast-iron casserole with a lid.

OTHER WAYS TO DECORATE

A third method consists of making decorated dough shapes, from plaits to baguettes, with cut strips, pretzels, croissants, flowers, hearts, etc. There are no limits to your imagination!

You can also draw or write on the dough. Prepare a mixture of dark cocoa, liquid sugar and water until just runny enough to be applied with a brush.

Using any of these methods, it is possible to make very nice gifts that will not only be beautiful, but also be tasty and healthy. Personally, I like to offer sourdough bread no matter what. I am delighted to see the happiness in the eyes of the receiver. Because good things are better when you share them.

SCORING PATTERNS

boule

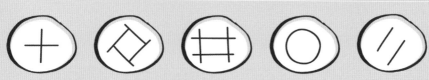

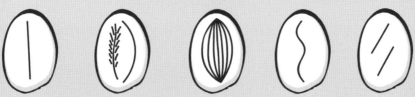

batard

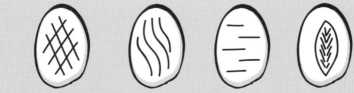

BAKE

For baking, you can choose between several possibilities. What you need most of all is a good oven. To obtain the effect of a bread oven, you can use a cast-iron casserole with a lid, which diffuses heat very well and retains the steam that the dough produces in the first 20 minutes. The disadvantage of such pots is that they are very heavy and you can only bake one loaf of bread at a time. The second possibility is to use an enamelled pot with a lid, which is lighter but also retains moisture well. You can also turn a high rimmed baking tin or other heat-resistant pot or pan over the dough. To bake several breads at the same time, I recommend using a steel plate or pizza steel or a granite, terracotta, fireclay or other baking stone. They are also perfect for baking pizzas, as their bottom is browned like that from a bread oven. A steel plate or pizza stone gives off heat very quickly, which is necessary in the first few minutes for the dough to rise during baking (oven spring), whereas baking stones keep the heat longer, but do not diffuse it as quickly. But to start with, an ordinary baking tray used in most home kitchens is perfectly sufficient. You may wish to consider purchasing one of the above-mentioned aids later on.

In any case, you must preheat the oven and the baking dish or tray to the highest temperature for at least 45 minutes before baking the dough. As far as I am concerned, I use a pizza steel or an enamelled pot. I preheat them for at least 45 minutes at 275°C/527°F. However, since all ovens are different, it is up to you to find the setting that suits you best. The recommended programme is that of natural convection: heating by the upper vault and the lower floor without ventilation. For steam generation in the oven, see the section on the next page, 'Steam in the oven, crusty bread on the table'. When baking the dough, lower the temperature to 230–240°C/445–460°F. This high temperature is essential during the first 15 minutes so that the dough, once sufficiently risen, can still rise in the oven. After 15 minutes, remove the lid or steam source to allow a crust to form on the surface of the dough and bake until the crust turns brown. One kilogram of dough should cook for 40–50 minutes in total. Rye bread requires more time and should be baked with steam for 15 minutes before lowering the temperature to 200°C/400°F and baking for another 50–60 minutes, depending on its size.

If you are using a cast-iron casserole, you can help yourself by turning the dough over on baking paper, then grasping the ends of the paper and placing the dough in the casserole. I use a small proving basket over which I can place the casserole, then I turn the basket over and remove it. The paper is handy if you want to bake the bread on a baking tray, as you only have to slide the dough on it with another baking tray. You can reuse the baking paper several times.

WHEN THE DOUGH IS BAKING

The processes in the dough accelerate when under the effect of heat and the enzymes work faster. During the last phase, the final rapid formation of carbon dioxide begins inside the dough, which spreads outwards so that the dough continues to grow. The enzymes on the surface of the dough become more active under the influence of heat and transform the starch into sugar-like compounds (dextrins), which contribute to the colouring of the crust at the end of the baking process. Yeast dies at an internal temperature of 55–60°C/131–140°F, just like bacteria. The gluten begins to coagulate and release water into the starch, which then sticks together to form the crumb. When the maximum temperature inside the bread is reached (90–100°C/194–212°F), the crust begins to colour.

At 100–177°C/212–350°F, the so-called Maillard reaction begins, where ketones, aldehydes and various acids are formed, which contribute to the taste and aroma. A nice brown crust depends mainly on this reaction, which also occurs when roasting meat. When the surface of the bread has a temperature of 149–204°C/300–399°F, the caramelisation of the remaining sugars in the crust is triggered, which contributes to the flavour (Hamelman, 2013). As a result, if the dough is too strongly fermented, the crust will remain pale because there is not enough sugar in the dough for the Maillard reaction. The same phenomenon occurs if there is no steam during the first 15 minutes of cooking.

STEAM IN THE OVEN, CRUSTY BREAD ON THE TABLE

The secret of obtaining a beautiful crispy, crust-like bread from a bakery is the addition of steam during the first 15 minutes of baking. The steam allows the bread to continue rising in the oven, as the steam makes its surface soft and smooth. If you don't use steam, the crust will become hard in contact with dry air and the dough will not rise. As a result, the bread will have less volume and a lighter crust.

There are several options for creating steam in your home oven:

1) Use a casserole with a lid, usually made of cast iron, that stores heat well. In my experience, an enamelled container is also quite appropriate. Both types of pots must be preheated in the oven for at least 45 minutes.

2) If you are baking on a baking tray, clay or steel plate or larger quantities at a time, place a smaller baking tin in the oven 15 minutes before putting the dough into it. Put a few ice cubes or pour boiling water into the tin when you put the dough into the oven.

3) Put lava stones in a smaller baking tin and heat in the oven. When you put the dough in it, pour boiling water on to the stones.

4) If you have a deeper baking tin, you can put it over the dough.

5) You can also apply moisture to the oven with a sprayer. I often use the smallest one that is used to spray plants.

6) Before baking, sprinkle the surface of the dough or moisten it with wet hands. This is usually not enough, but still better than nothing.

7) Use a steam combi oven that automatically provides the right amount of steam for cooking.

After 15 minutes of steaming, remove the lid or baking tin with water to allow the crust to finish baking perfectly. If you want a softer crust, leave the steam in the oven a little longer.

If the dough contains a lot of sugar, butter or eggs (brioche, croissants, etc.), there is no need to steam it.

For me, the oven is the heart of the kitchen, and without it nothing can be done. I confess that I have always wished for a high-quality oven in my kitchen, and last year that wish came true. Since the end of August 2019, I have been testing and using the Miele H 7860 BP steam oven* with great pleasure. Its characteristics appeal to me because it offers everything I need to cook excellent sourdough dishes. In my old oven, I regularly burned myself with hot water when I wanted to generate steam in the oven, at the beginning of cooking or after 15 minutes when I had to remove the water from the oven. I don't have these problems with the Miele oven because it has a unique steam-cooking programme. The crust of the bread is even more beautiful than before, even crispier and of a magnificent colour. I would like to give you another tip for a crispier crust: turn the fan on during the last 10 minutes of baking. I chose the Miele steam oven because it adds steam even at 275°C/527°F, whereas conventional ovens only add steam up to 230°C/446°F. A high initial temperature is important for the dough to rise during baking; of course, it must have been proved well. This

*The oven was supplied to me by Miele Slovenia. I am giving my personal and sincere opinion here because I can recommend it without any hesitation.

oven is easy to use and allows you to adjust the amount of steam and cooking time. I can follow the baking process with a camera mounted above the oven if I am not always at home. The oven has a built-in timer, which is sometimes useful because I can set the time I want to preheat it in the evening. It saves having to get up early in the morning. I never thought I would be able to clean the oven so effectively by pyrolysis after baking sourdough pizzas and other sourdough products with toppings. From now on, I'll cook even more often.

COOLING AND SLICING THE BREAD

When the aromas from the oven are delightful and the crust turns a beautiful dark or golden brown, it's time to take the bread out. Place it on a rack so that air can circulate around it and the underside remains dry, otherwise it will become soft and damp. As it cools, the moisture moves from the crumb to the crust. For a crispy crust, do not cover the bread. If you prefer a soft crust, steam the oven a little longer or brush the crust with butter or oil after baking. You can also cover the bread with a slightly dampened cloth or wrap it in a towel.

If you can control yourself long enough not to eat the bread while it is still warm, wait until it has cooled before slicing it. Only then does the taste and aroma develop beautifully and the crumb becomes nice and firm. It should therefore cool after cooking for at least 1 hour, but preferably 2 hours. Rye bread must rest for at least 12 hours, or even 24 hours. This is the time it takes for the rye crumb to firm up and develop its flavour – rye bread ages well and improves even with time.

When I slice the bread, I place it on a board with the cut side down for the first 2 days and usually wrap it in a linen bread bag as well. After 2 days, I put everything in a plastic bag to prevent it drying out. At home, the shelf life of a loaf of bread is not important, because I make smaller loaves that are eaten in 2 or 3 days. This allows me to bake more often.

OTHER METHODS

This section lists procedures that are different from the general procedure.

100 PER CENT RYE

Recipes for both types of bread can be found on pages 148 and 149. Here, however, both procedures are also illustrated.

EASY RYE TIN LOAF

Mix the flour and water with a spatula or wooden spoon to obtain a mixture similar to very soft clay. Leave it to rest for 20 minutes, then add the starter (which has doubled in size) and salt. Mix until all ingredients are well combined and distributed throughout the mixture. Cover and mix again after 20 minutes. Grease or oil the loaf tin and transfer the mixture to the tin with a spatula. Dust with plenty of rye flour and leave to rest, uncovered, for 2 hours. Then cover it with a shower cap or linen or cotton cloth to prevent the dough drying out. Leave to rise until the dough has doubled in size and the surface is well cracked, exactly like a loaf of rye bread.

 TIP

Sourdoughs tend to be more acidic with rye. Even when they collapse a little, they're still active. Due to the nature of rye flour, the dough must be more acidic. If you ever have too much sourdough left over that you can't use with other types of flour, you can still use this sourdough in the preparation of rye bread. Keep in mind that the rye dough will be very sticky, which is absolutely normal.

RYE BOULE

Mix the flour and almost all of the water with a spatula or wooden spoon to obtain a crumbly mixture. Leave to rest for 20 minutes, then add the starter (which has doubled in size), residual water and salt. Mix until all ingredients are well combined and distributed throughout the mixture. Cover for 20 minutes, then mix or knead the dough again.

Dust the work surface with plenty of rye flour, then put the rye dough on it. Dust your hands with flour well and form the loaf into a round shape by folding the dough. Roll it in rye flour and place it in a floured basket or just on a tray, as I usually do. Dust a large amount of rye flour over the top.

If the dough is placed on a tray, do not cover it for 1 hour 30 minutes, then cover it with a deep baking tin or dish so that it does not dry out. If in a basket, tie a shower cap, linen cloth or cling film over it. Leave to stand until double in volume and the surface is well cracked.

RYE BEFORE
RISING

RYE
BREAD
BEFORE
BAKING

BAGUETTE

To preshape a baguette, form a square of dough and roll it up towards you. As you roll it, gently press the dough away from you. When done, leave it on the top seam-side down. Lightly dust with flour and cover with a cloth. Leave it to stand, covered, for at least 20 minutes.

Turn the dough for the final shaping so that the smooth side is facing upwards. You can repeat this operation by forming it into a sausage, or folding the two top edges inwards. Then fold the upper part in half. Turn the dough 180 degrees. Fold the two top edges inwards again and fold the upper part in half, using your thumb.

Fold the top half over the bottom half and press evenly with your thumb or lower part of your palm on the dough. (Cont. on page 125)

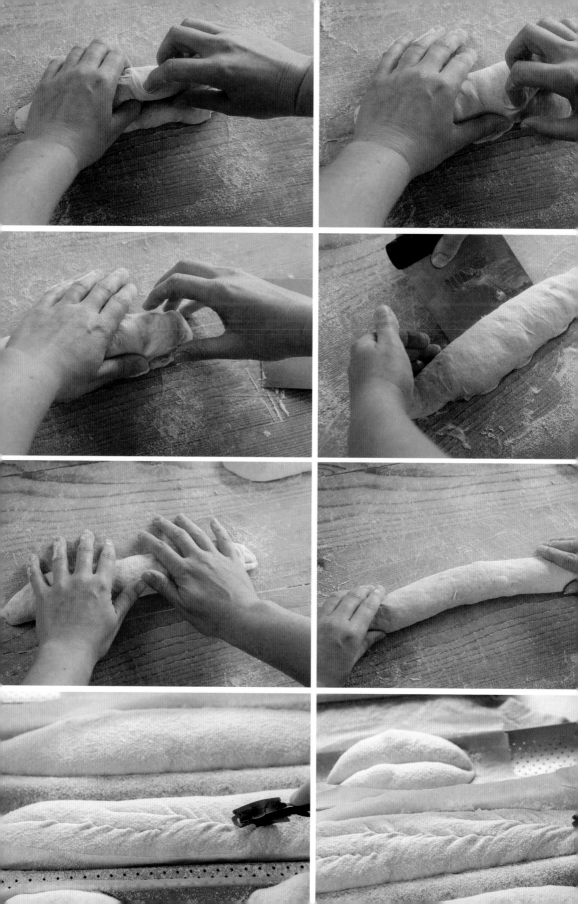

Roll the dough with your hands until you reach the length you want for a baguette.

If your dough resists shaping, cover it and leave it to rest for about 10 minutes. Then roll the baguette to the desired length.

Put it on a baking tray with the seam down. When properly proved, use a razor blade to score three times in the middle so that the incisions overlap by one third.

DOUGH BALLS

Some bakery products are shaped only once, such as dough balls for rolls or doughnuts and the like. Grasp a piece of dough with your lightly floured hand and fold all the edges inwards. For doughnuts, put the filling in the middle of the dough and fold the edges down.

Then form round pieces on the work surface by grasping them with the palm of your hand and making circular motions to create friction between the piece of dough, the palm of your hand and the work surface. Smaller round shapes can also be easily formed in the palms of the hands by creating friction between the dough and the palm. Flour them.

PIZZA

To make a pizza, first make dough balls and leave them to stand, covered, for at least 20 minutes. Then you can shape the dough with the back of your hand and your fingers or form a border with your fingers and stretch the dough outwards. Do not roll out the dough with a rolling pin, as this will remove bubbles, which is not desirable. If you can't shape the dough, leave it to rest, covered, for at least 10–15 minutes. Meanwhile, the gluten will relax, allowing you to shape it more easily.

Do not put too much topping on the pizza, so that it cooks well and quickly. The dough will remain crispy and the filling juicy.

During the actual baking process, it is important to bake the pizza at the highest possible temperature in the preheated oven. Personally, I use a cooking method with the top of the oven at 275°C/527°F, or as hot as your oven will go. In my experience, the ideal is to use a pizza stone, where it will cook in 10–12 minutes. You can also use a fireclay baking stone or an ordinary upturned baking tray that you have preheated at the same time as the oven. Then simply slide the pizza on with baking paper.

MAKING PUFF PASTRY

Puff pastry is used for croissants and Danish pastries.

CROISSANTS AND DANISH PASTRY

Make the dough as indicated on page 224 or page 220. Before rolling, the dough must be brought to room temperature, which takes about 45 minutes (at 21°C/69°F). Meanwhile, prepare a 20-cm square of butter. The dough and the butter square should be at about the same temperature. The butter should be kneadable but not too soft, otherwise it should be put in the freezer for 5 minutes. On a lightly floured surface, roll out the dough into a square roughly 30 x 30 cm. It is larger than the butter square, so you can wrap the butter in it like an envelope. Seal the dough well around the butter so that it does not leak. (Cont. on page 132)

For croissants, fold three times into a letter shape, or once into a letter shape and once into a book shape. For Danish pastries, fold three times into a letter shape. After finishing the folds, wrap the dough in cling film and place in the refrigerator for 30 minutes. When you take it out of the refrigerator, turn it 90 degrees before rolling it up so that the edge where the dough is folded is facing you. Fold down again to form a 60-cm long rectangle. After the last folding, wrap the dough again in cling film and keep it in the refrigerator until the next day.

Letter folds

Roll the square into a 60-cm rectangle.

Fold the top two thirds of the rectangle towards you, then fold the bottom over the top. (Cont. on page 135)

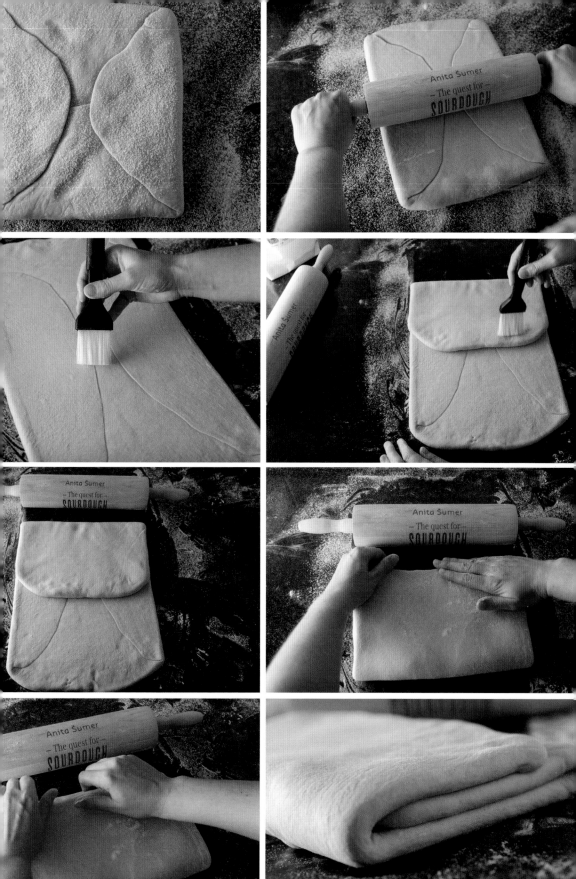

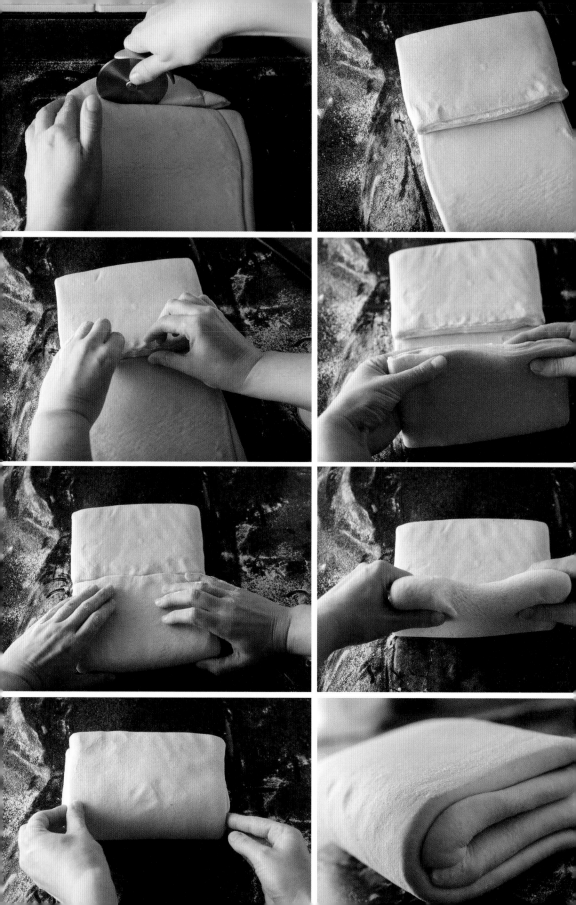

Book fold

Fold the top half of the rectangle in half, as well as the bottom half. Then fold the bottom over the top.

If the edges are not straight, you can cut and join them again.

Shaping croissants

For croissants, roll the dough on the next day into a rectangle 0.4-cm thick, 20-cm wide and 110-cm long. If the dough resists rolling, cover it and leave it to rest for 10 minutes. Cut it into triangles and roll them into croissants. As you roll the dough, you can slightly stretch the thin end of the triangle with your fingers before forming a croissant. Lay them on a tray and coat with the egg glaze (see page 224). Cover them with cling film and leave to rise until doubled in size. Brush them again before baking.

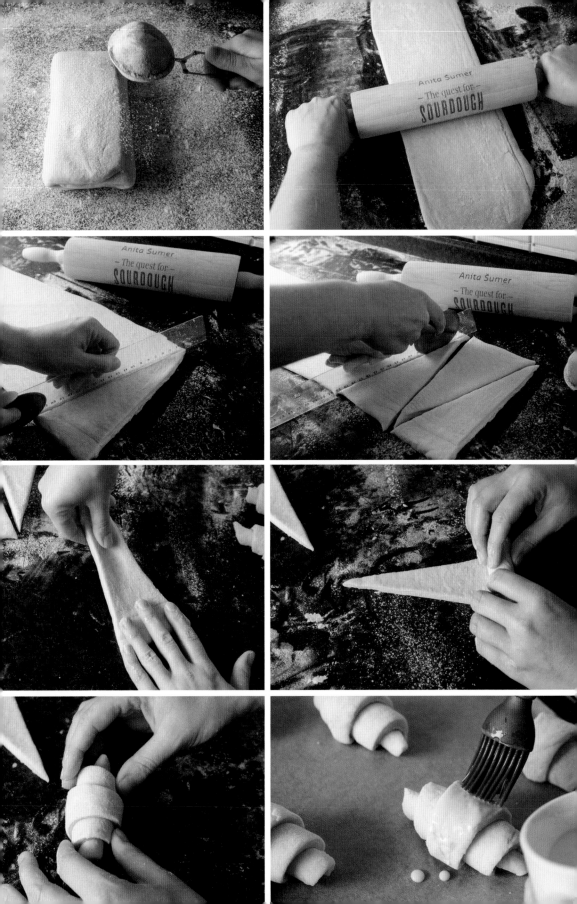

Shaping Danish pastries

For Danish pastries, roll out the dough on the next day into a rectangle 0.4-cm thick, 20-cm wide and 110-cm long. Trim the edges, cut the dough into squares and make into different shapes.

DON'T FORGET: BEFORE BAKING WITH A STARTER

1. LET'S MAKE AND PREPARE THE STARTER

2. FLOUR BECOMES BREAD

3. STEP-BY-STEP DOUGH PREPARATION

LET'S MAKE AND PREPARE THE STARTER

- Always feed the mother starter with the same type of flour.
- Don't use different starters, one is enough.
- A starter should be soft, bubbly and smell like yoghurt before use. It should double in size after the last feeding.

FLOUR BECOMES BREAD

- Do not mix too many different types of flour. Start with white plain flour or rye flour. See page 43.
- Always add water gradually.

STEP-BY-STEP DOUGH PREPARATION

- Watch the dough, not the clock. Use all your senses when baking with sourdough.
- If you are short on time, you can mix all the ingredients: flour, water, salt and starter at the same time, knead well and omit the stretching and folding step.

BAKING SCHEDULES

- The starter does not need to be fed daily. When not in use, feed it, leave it for 1 hour and then refrigerate, where it will keep for at least 1 week.
- Sourdough baking can be perfectly integrated in your daily routine. To do this, follow the 'Baking Schedules' section on page 273.

SOURDOUGH RECIPES

- Use the same recipe several times before experimenting. Rye flour and wheat flour are ideal choices for an introduction to sourdough baking.
- The recipe does not have to be followed to the letter. You can also add more or less starter.
- Adjust the speed of fermentation to the amount of sourdough added. Room temperature and ingredients influence this speed. The higher the temperature, the faster the dough will ferment.
- There should be at least 15 hours between kneading and baking. In this case, the dough should be refrigerated for a certain period of time.

USEFUL ADVICE FOR MAKING SOURDOUGH

- If your sourdough is acidic, take 5 g and put it into another clean jar. Add 15 g of water and 20 g of flour. Allow the mixture to double in volume. Repeat if necessary.
- You will find many answers to your questions in the chapter 'Starter SOS' on page 254.

AND THE MOST IMPORTANT TIP

Savour the time you invest in baking your bread: it is the prelude to a rich and delicious return.

Sourdough recipes

I have selected my favourite recipes. Most of them also provide suggestions for other delicious variations.

The quantities of water and other liquids are only approximate. It's up to you to get to know the flour you're working with and adjust the amounts of water or other liquids if necessary. Always start with less water (reduce by 5 per cent or more) in recipes for bread and bakes; you can always add the difference after autolysis and during the second kneading. If, instead of using the leaven, you use your starter directly with 100 per cent hydration, also reduce the amount of water in the dough (about 5 per cent less). All recipes for which nothing is specified can be made using the basic method described on pages 78–114.

You can also estimate the quantities approximately: 2 teaspoons of flour weighs about 20 g, 2 teaspoons water about 10 g, 1 teaspoon salt about 4–5 g. Nevertheless, the use of digital kitchen scales is highly recommended. Since all ovens differ from each other and do not bake all the same, the stated baking times are only indicative.

I hope you will enjoy discovering the recipes and savouring all these delights. Time is an important element in sourdough baking, so bake with peace of mind. The dough will work for you – just look at it, touch it, feel it, forget the clock and be patient. If you don't get it right the first time, just start over and take notes while you work. Repeat a recipe several times until successful. If you change the recipes later, change only one item at a time. Naturally, even in baking, practice makes perfect!

Bread
and bread
products

EASY RYE TIN LOAF

No need to worry when it comes to rye bread: it is certainly the simplest bread to start and learn about sourdough baking. It does not need to be kneaded and can be prepared fairly quickly. But there's a slight snag: you have to wait at least 12 hours (and ideally 24 hours) until it has cooled down, the crumb is firm and the taste has fully developed – but I assure you it's well worth it.

LEAVEN:

10 g active starter (3%)
35 g rye flour (10%)
35 g water (10%)

Mix the ingredients, cover and wait until doubled in size.

MAIN DOUGH:

(for a 22 x 10.5 x 7-cm loaf tin)
350 g rye flour (100%)
330 g water (95%)
7 g salt (2%)

Mix the flour and water with a spatula or wooden spoon to obtain a mixture similar to very soft clay. Leave it to rest for 20 minutes, then add the leaven (doubled in size) and salt. Mix until all ingredients are well combined and distributed throughout the mixture. Cover and mix well again after 20 minutes. Grease or oil the loaf tin and transfer the mixture to it with a spatula. Dust with plenty of rye flour and leave to rise, uncovered, for 2 hours. Then cover it with a shower cap or linen or cotton cloth to prevent the dough drying out. Allow to rise until the dough has doubled in size and the surface is well cracked. Bake as directed on pages 111–114. After 15 minutes, lower the temperature to 200°C/400°F/gas 6 and bake for a further 40–50 minutes for 800 grams of bread.

TIP

Use wet fingers to distribute the mixture in the baking tin, making it easier to distribute the rye mixture without it clinging to your hands, or wetting the spatula. With rye flour, it takes a while for the starter to begin to work, and then the mixture doubles fairly quickly. So follow the dough. You can also add 10-20 per cent rye seeds or grains previously soaked overnight and drained.

RYE BOULE

Now that you know a little more about working rye flour, you're ready to make real rye bread! It's not difficult, but this time you'll have to use your hands and a work surface for shaping a round loaf, or boule. The ingredients are almost the same as those of the quick version, but a little less water is needed.

LEAVEN:

10 g active starter (2.5%)
40 g rye flour (10%)
50 g water (12.5%)

Mix the ingredients, cover and wait until doubled in size.

MAIN DOUGH:

400 g rye flour (100%)
300 g water (75%)
8 g salt (2%)

Mix the flour and 280 g of water with a spatula or wooden spoon to obtain a crumbly mixture. Leave to rest for 20 minutes, then add the leaven (doubled in size), 20 g of water and salt. Mix until all ingredients are well combined and distributed throughout the mixture. Cover and mix well again after 20 minutes. Dust the work surface with plenty of rye flour, then place the rye dough on it. Generously dust your hands with flour and shape the loaf into a round by folding it. Roll it in rye flour and place it in a floured basket or simply on a tray, like I do myself. Dust the top generously with plenty of rye flour. If placed on a tray, leave to rise, uncovered for 1 hour 30 minutes, then cover it with a deep baking tin so that it does not dry out. If in a basket, tie a shower cap, linen cloth or cling film over it. It should prove so long that it doubles in size and the surface to be cracked nicely. Bake as directed on pages 111–114. After 15 minutes, lower the temperature to 200°C/400°F/gas 6 and bake for another 40-50 minutes for 800 grams of bread.

TIP

Cumin, coriander and anise go well in rye bread. You can add them at the same time as the leaven and salt. These spices will further enhance its taste. The recommended amount is 1–2 per cent, depending on taste.

BREAD IN A FLASH

This strong flour-based bread is prepared according to a specific principle that consists of using one part of active ingredients for every two parts of water and three parts of flour. You can also use a combination of other flour types, but white plain flour and strong white flour are the most suitable. For spelt flour, reduce the water content by 10 per cent, for rye and wholemeal flour, add about 5 per cent water. Because of the greater amount of starter in the recipe, the bread will also rise more quickly.

100 g active starter (33%)
200 g water (66%)
300 g strong white (type 812) flour (100%)
6 g salt (2%)

Mix the flour and water to obtain a smooth mixture. Leave it to rest for at least 20 minutes, then add the starter and salt. Knead well to make sure all ingredients are incorporated and form a dough. Knead two or three times for 2–3 minutes each. In the next 2 hours, make at least four sets of stretch and folds (see page 89) every 20–30 minutes.

Wait for the dough to double in size. Preshape the loaf, rest it on the work surface, then do the final shape and place it in the flour-dusted banneton (see pages 92–105). When it has doubled in size, bake it in a preheated oven. The baking instructions can be found on pages 111–114.

WHITE BREAD

As has already been mentioned, it is easiest for a beginner to bake with white plain flour as it contains good gluten-forming proteins. Now it's your turn to knead white bread.

LEAVEN:

10 g active starter (2%)
50 g strong white (type 812) flour (10%)
40 g water (8%)

Mix the ingredients, cover and wait until doubled in size.

MAIN DOUGH:

500 g strong white (type 812) flour (100%)
325 g water (65%)
10 g salt (2%)

Mix the flour and water into a smooth mixture, leave to stand, covered, for at least 20 minutes and then add the leaven and salt. Knead vigorously so that all the ingredients are incorporated and form a dough. Knead two or three times for 2–3 minutes each time. Over the next 2 hours, stretch and fold at least four times every 20–30 minutes (see page 89). Shape and bake following the instructions on pages 94-114.

 TIP

You can add presoaked seeds to this dough (up to 15 per cent, depending on the weight of the flour). Subtract the amount of water in which you soak the seeds from the amount of water indicated in the recipe. If the dough is too dry, you can add water. For instructions on adding seeds, see page 74.

SUNDAY MORNING MILK BREAD

The smell of freshly baked bread will get sleepy heads out of bed in the morning, even at dawn! The preparation requires a little elbow grease, but the softness of this bread will be a real reward.

LEAVEN:

10 g active starter *(2.5%)*
40 g strong white (type 812) flour *(10%)*
30 g water *(7.5%)*

Mix the ingredients, cover and wait until doubled in size.

MAIN DOUGH:
(for a 22 x 10.5 x 7-cm loaf tin)

400 g strong white (type 812) flour *(100%)*
280 g milk *(70%)*
20 g soft brown sugar *(5%)*
8 g salt *(2%)*
20 g room temperature butter *(5%)*

GLAZE:

1 tablespoon milk
1 tablespoon cream

First mix the flour and 260 g of milk and leave it to rest for at least 20 minutes. Then add the salt and sugar in 20 g of milk along with the leaven. Mix well so that all the ingredients combine into a smooth dough. Knead for at least 5 minutes.

Leave it to rest, covered, for 20 minutes, then gradually add the butter and rub it into the dough – this will be easier to do on the work surface. After adding the butter, knead the dough well for a further 5 minutes. You can also use the technique of slapping and folding. The dough must then be left to rest again for a further 15 minutes. Knead again vigorously for at least 5 minutes.

Cover and let rise until the dough has increased by about half. Then slide it onto a lightly oiled work surface and degas by hand to obtain small and regular holes. Roll the dough into a sausage.

Place the loaf in a greased loaf tin. Cover it with cling film and leave to rise again. Before baking, coat it with a mixture of cream and milk. Bake with steam for the first 15 minutes in a preheated oven at 200°C/400°F/gas 6, then bake until the crust is evenly browned, usually 35–40 minutes.

After baking, brush the bread with butter to soften the crust.

TIP

For vegan bread, replace the cow's milk with a vegan alternative. Instead of butter, use olive oil and reduce the amount of milk by the amount of oil used (by 20 g). The secret to a soft crumb is long kneading.

WHITE WITH A TOUCH OF RYE

LEAVEN:

10 g active starter (2%)
40 g strong white (type 812) flour (8%)
10 g rye flour (2%)
40 g water (8%)

Mix the ingredients, cover and wait until doubled in size.

MAIN DOUGH:

100 g rye flour (20%)
400 g strong white (type 812) flour (80%)
360 g water (72%)
10 g salt (2%)

Mix the flour and water into a smooth mixture, leave to rest, cover for at least 20 minutes, then add the leaven and salt. Knead vigorously so that all the ingredients are incorporated and form a dough. After a brief rest, knead two or three times for 2–3 minutes each time. Over the next 2 hours, stretch and fold at least four times every 20–30 minutes (see page 89) every 20–30 minutes. Shape and bake following the instructions on pages 94–114.

EINKORN AND SPELT LOAF

LEAVEN:

20 g active starter *(5%)*
55 g water *(14%)*
30 g einkorn flour *(7.5%)*
30 g spelt flour *(7.5%)*

Mix the ingredients, cover and wait for their volume to double.

MAIN DOUGH:
(for a 22 x 10.5 x 7-cm loaf tin)

200 g einkorn flour *(50%)*
200 g spelt flour *(50%)*
250 g water *(62.5%)*

Olive oil

Mix 200 g of einkorn flour and 200 g of water and leave to stand for 30 minutes. Then add 200 g spelt flour and 50 g water. After 20 minutes, add all the leaven and 8 g of salt. Knead everything well, then stretch and fold three times in 2 hours. Knead gently, without excess force. The size of the dough must increase by half. Oil the work surface with 2 tablespoons of olive oil, place the dough over it and roll into a sausage. Place this dough in a greased loaf tin and leave to rise until doubled in size.

Bake with steam in a preheated oven at 240°C/475°F/gas 9 for 15 minutes, then bake for a further 40-45 minutes.

YELLOW CORN BREAD

LEAVEN:

20 g active starter *(3.6%)*
60 g strong white (type 812) flour *(11%)*
40 g water *(7.3%)*

Mix the ingredients, cover and wait for their volume to double.

MAIN DOUGH:

150 g corn flour *(27%)*
400 g strong white (type 812) flour *(73%)*
50 g polenta *(9%)*
580 g water *(105%)*
12 g salt *(2%)*

Polenta for rolling

Brown the corn flour and polenta in a dry pan until they emit a nice aroma, pour 400 g of boiling water over them and mix quickly and thoroughly to obtain a dense mixture. After the mixture has cooled, add 400 g of strong flour, mix vigorously, then gradually add 120 g of water, knead well and gradually add a further 60 g of water. If the dough becomes too sticky, do not add more water. Knead into a smooth dough. After 20 minutes, add 120 g of leaven and 12 g of salt and knead. After a short rest, knead two times for 2 minutes. Over the next 2 hours, make four sets of stretches and folds every 20–30 minutes (see page 89). Shape and bake following the instructions on pages 94–114.

🫙 **TIP**

Don't be alarmed by the structure of the dough, as it is perfectly normal for it to be a little sticky and will stick to hands due to the steamed maize flour and polenta. Over time, the dough will become more pliable and easier to shape. You can put it in the fridge for about an hour before shaping. For a softer crumb, you can replace half the water with milk.

DURUM WHEAT BREAD

This tasty yellow crumb is an absolute delight, even when the sun is not shining.

LEAVEN:

25 g active starter (5%)
80 g durum wheat flour (16%)
70 g water (14%)

Mix the ingredients, cover and wait until doubled in size.

MAIN DOUGH:

500 g durum wheat flour (100%; if you have a grinder at home, grind it again)
350 g water (70%)
10 g salt (2%)
Olive oil

Mix the flour and water into a smooth mixture, cover and leave to rest for 8 hours or refrigerate overnight. Add the leaven and salt and knead the dough. After a brief rest, knead two or three times for 2–3 minutes. Over the next 2 hours, make five sets of stretches and folds every 20–30 minutes (see page 89). Add 10 g of water (1.6%) to the first and second sets of stretches and folds. Shape and bake following the instructions on pages 94–114. The final proving should take place in the refrigerator.

DARK BEER BREAD

LEAVEN:

10 g active starter (2%)
50 g strong white (type 812) flour (10%)
40 g water (8%)

Mix the ingredients, cover and wait until doubled in size.

MAIN DOUGH:

500 g strong white (type 812) flour (100%)
340 g dark beer stout (68%; I use Oyster Stout)
10 g salt (2%)

Slowly add the beer to the flour and mix to obtain a smooth mixture. Leave to rest, covered, for 1 hour 30 minutes, then add leaven and salt and knead well into the dough. After a brief rest, knead two or three times for 2–3 minutes. You can also use the technique of slapping and folding. Over the next 2 hours, make five sets of stretches and folds (see page 89). Shape and bake following the instructions on pages 94–114. The final proving should take place in the refrigerator.

 TIP

If you do not bake bread straight from the refrigerator, put it into the fridge for at least 1 hour before baking to firm up.

SOURDOUGH PIZZA

If you've never had sourdough pizza before, there's none better! A crispy crust, a tender, open crumb, topped to order, aromatic and delicious – in fact just like all sourdough preparations.

LEAVEN:

10 g active starter (2%)
50 g strong white (type 812) flour (10%)
40 g water (8%)

Mix the ingredients, cover and wait until doubled in size.

MAIN DOUGH:

(for 2-3 pizzas)
460 g strong white (type 812) flour (92%)
40 g wholemeal flour (8%)
330 g water (66%)
10 g salt (2%)

Mix all the flours and 300 g of water (60%) to obtain a smooth mixture and cover. After 1 hour, add 30 g of water, 10 g of salt and 100 g of leaven and mix well. I usually make this dough on a Wednesday night so I can eat pizza on a Saturday. I then leave the dough in the fridge overnight (no stretching and folding). The next morning, I wait for the dough to warm to room temperature, and then make four sets of stretches and folds in 2 hours (see page 89), leave it at room temperature for 2–3 hours, then put the dough back in the refrigerator until Friday afternoon, when I take it out again for 3 hours. Finally, I put it back in the fridge until Saturday morning. The dough should be nicely bubbly before being used. Of course, you can do this process in a day or two, but the taste will probably be different. For more information, see page 128.

 TIP

Adjust the baking schedule to your own needs. You can, for example, take the dough out of the refrigerator for the first time when you come back home from work, stretch and fold it several times, let it rest for 2–3 hours, then put it back in the refrigerator. The pizza will be even tastier if you roll cottage cheese or ricotta cheese into the rim. This dough can be kept for a long time in the refrigerator.

DURUM FOCACCIA WITH ROSEMARY AND GARLIC

In the region of Provence in France this is known as *fougasse*.

LEAVEN:

50 g active starter (10%)
50 g water (10%)
50 g durum wheat flour (10%)

Mix the ingredients, cover and wait until doubled in size.

MAIN DOUGH:

500 g durum wheat flour (100%)
375 g water (75%)
10 g salt (2%)

Olive oil, rosemary, garlic to taste and desire

Mix the flour and water into a smooth mixture and leave to stand for 8 hours or overnight in the refrigerator. The next morning, add the leaven and 10 g of salt (2%), then knead well to obtain a dough. After a brief rest, knead two or three times for 2–3 minutes. Over the next 2 hours, make at least five sets of stretches and folds every 20–30 minutes (see page 89). Leave to rise until doubled in size, then put into a baking tray, make indents with your fingers, drizzle with olive oil and arrange the rosemary and chopped garlic over the surface. Leave to rise until doubled in size. Bake without steam at 230°C/450°F/gas 8 for 20–30 minutes until nicely brown in colour.

TIP

You can also use strong white flour or plain flour or up to half wholemeal flour and other combinations of spices, herbs, cherry tomatoes, cheese, dried tomatoes, etc., or you can top it with pieces of bacon.

BUCKWHEAT BREAD WITH WALNUTS

Buckwheat and walnuts, a classic combination that practically turns this bread into a dessert.

LEAVEN:

10 g active starter (2%)
45 g strong white (type 812) flour (9%)
45 g water (9%)

Mix the ingredients, cover and wait until doubled in size.

MAIN DOUGH:

100 g buckwheat flour (20%)
400 g strong white (type 812) flour (80%)
450 g water (90%)
10 g salt (2%)
100 g roasted walnuts, cooled and chopped (20%)

Toast the buckwheat flour in a dry casserole dish until it emits an aroma. Remove from the heat, add 200 g of boiling water and mix well. Transfer the mixture into a bowl to knead the dough in and leave it to cool slightly. Add 150 g of water and stir gently to dissolve any lumps. Add the strong flour and start kneading with your hands. Gradually add the rest of the water; if the dough starts to seem too runny, stop adding water. The dough should be soft, slightly sticky, but still kneadable. Cover and leave to rest for at least 30 minutes. Then add the leaven and salt and knead to a perfectly smooth dough. After a short rest, knead two times for 2 minutes. Over the next 2 hours, make four sets of stretches and folds (see page 89), then add nuts in a third set. Put the dough into the refrigerator overnight or leave it to rise by 60–70 per cent. After shaping the bread, roll it in buckwheat flour and leave it to rise in a basket. Leave to rise and bake according to the instructions on pages 94–114.

 TIP

For a stronger buckwheat taste, use up to a third of buckwheat flour, in which case increase the amount of water if necessary. You can also replace half the water with milk.

CIABATTA

Traditional Italian bread with an open crumb, shaped like a slipper (It. *ciabatta*).

LEAVEN:

10 g active starter *(2.5%)*
25 g strong white (type 812) flour *(6%)*
25 g water *(6%)*

Mix the ingredients, cover and wait until doubled in size.

MAIN DOUGH:

350 g strong white (type 812) flour *(87%)*
50 g manitoba wheat flour *(13%)*
300 g water *(75%)*
8 g salt *(2%)*
10 g olive oil *(2.5%)*

Mix the two types of flour and then gradually add the water, starting with 260 g. When the flour has been completely absorbed, add another 20 g. Cover the dough and leave to stand for at least 30 minutes. Stir in the leaven, salt and 10 g of water, then knead. Then slowly add the remaining 10 g of water for the next kneading. Leave to rest for 10 minutes, then fold the dough well with the scooping and stretching technique on page 87. Now is also a good time to add the olive oil as the gluten is already well developed.

Over the next 2–3 hours, leave the dough to rise and make four sets of stretches and folds (see page 89). Put the dough into the refrigerator for at least 8 hours. Before shaping, leave it to rise until doubled in size so that it is full of small bubbles before shaping. Turn the dough over and cut it to form four small 'cushions' or two larger shapes. When shaping, take care so the bubbles remain in the dough. Fold the cut edges of the cut pieces under the dough. Leave to rise again until the ciabattas rise well and are puffy. Bake according to the baking instructions on pages 111–114.

WHOLEMEAL BREAD

LEAVEN:

10 g active starter *(2%)*
25 g wholemeal spelt flour *(5%)*
25 g strong white (type 812) flour *(5%)*
40 g water *(8%)*

Mix the ingredients, cover and wait until doubled in size.

MAIN DOUGH:

250 g wholemeal spelt flour *(50%)*
250 g strong white (type 812) flour *(50%)*
350 g water *(70%)*
10 g salt *(2%)*

Mix the wholemeal spelt flour with 250 g of water to a smooth mixture, cover and leave to rest for 30 minutes. Then add the white flour and gradually stir in 80 g of water. Mix and knead gently, then leave to rest for 20 minutes. Add the leaven and salt and gradually a further 20 g of water and knead. After a brief rest, knead two or three times for 3 minutes.

Over the next 2 hours, perform five sets of stretches and folds (see page 89). Then follow the instructions for rising, shaping and baking on pages 94–114. Before preshaping, you can refrigerate the dough for 1 hour to make it easier to shape. After the final shaping, leave the basket for about 2 hours at room temperature, then put it into the refrigerator. Put the bread in the oven straight from the refrigerator when it has risen sufficiently.

TIP

If the flour permits, add another 20 g (4%) of water during the third kneading, which you can incorporate by gently pressing the dough (see page 84). You can also use wholemeal wheat flour instead of wholemeal spelt flour. If you prefer, you can also use white spelt flour instead of white wheat flour, in which case use one tenth less water.

SPELT BREAD VARIATION

I came up with the idea for this bread because the dough spreads too much when using only spelt flour, even though I used less water. This recipe succeeds every time.

LEAVEN:

10 g active starter (2%)
25 g wholemeal spelt flour (5%)
25 g white spelt flour (5%)
40 g water (8%)

Mix the ingredients, cover and wait until doubled in size.

MAIN DOUGH:

250 g wholemeal spelt flour (50%)
250 g white spelt flour (50%)
400 g water (80%)
15 g psyllium husks (3%)
10 g salt (2%)

Mix 250 g of wholemeal spelt flour with 250 g of water and leave to stand, covered, for 20 minutes. Soak the psyllium husks in 80 g of water, stirring well to ensure they swell. Then add the psyllium husks, white spelt flour and 50 g of water. Leave it to stand for at least 20 minutes. After autolysis, add the leaven, 20 g of water and salt. Knead well. After a brief rest, knead two or three times for 2 minutes. Over the next 2 hours, make four sets of stretches and folds (see page 89). Leave to rise until the dough has doubled in size. Shape and bake following the instructions on pages 94–114.

CRUSTY BAGUETTE

LEAVEN:

10 g active starter (2.5%)
40 g strong white (type 812) flour (10%)
30 g water (7.5%)

Mix the ingredients, cover and wait until doubled in size.

MAIN DOUGH:

350 g strong white (type 812) flour (87%)
50 g wholemeal flour (13%)
260 g water (65%)
8 g salt (2%)

Mix all the flour and water to obtain a smooth mixture and leave to stand for 1 hour. Add the leaven and salt, then knead well. After a brief rest, knead two or three times for 2–3 minutes. Over the next 2 hours, make five sets of stretches and folds (see page 89). Leave the dough on the work surface, covered, to rise for a further hour, then refrigerate for 8 hours or overnight. The next day, take the dough out of the refrigerator and leave it to rise until doubled in size. You can then refrigerate it for about 1 hour to make it easier to shape the baguettes. Make three baguettes as described on pages 122–125 and place them on baking paper, in a baguette baking tin or in the folds of a floured cloth (with the seam facing upwards). Cover and leave to rise again until the baguettes are almost double in size and are nicely bubbly and taut. Score them before baking in an oven with steam preheated to 240°C/475°F/gas 9 for 10 minutes, then without steam for 10-15 minutes until golden brown.

🫙 TIP

Allow the baguettes to cool, then slice them, fill with thin rounds of home-made garlic butter, wrap in kitchen foil and bake in the oven at 240°C/475°F/gas 9 for about 15 minutes, then open the foil on top and bake for another 5 minutes. For home-made garlic butter, you need 200 g of butter, a head of garlic, a few sprigs of parsley and salt. Melt 2 tablespoons of butter and mix with the garlic and salt in a blender, then add the remaining butter and mix well, place in cling film and roll into a sausage. Put the butter into the fridge until it hardens.

BREAD ROLLS

For breakfast, a snack or great home-made sandwiches.

LEAVEN:

10 g active starter (2.5%)
30 g strong white (type 812) flour (7.5%)
20 g wholemeal flour (2.5%)
40 g water (7.5%)

Mix the ingredients, cover and wait until doubled in size.

MAIN DOUGH:
(for about nine medium-sized rolls)

450 g strong white (type 812) flour (90%)
50 g wholemeal flour (10%)
120 g cold milk (24%)
180 g water (36%)
15 g soft brown sugar (3%)
10 g salt (2%)
20 g olive or sunflower oil (4%)

Pour 100 g of boiling water over the wholemeal flour. Stir well until all the flour is absorbed, then add the cold milk and remaining water and mix again to obtain a medium-thick mixture. Sift the white flour into a stand mixer bowl and gradually add the flour, milk and water mixture and mix at the lowest speed until all ingredients are well combined into the dough. Cover and leave to rest for at least 30 minutes.

Meanwhile, mix in the oil, salt and sugar. After autolysis, add the leaven and the oil, salt and sugar mixture. Knead until the dough no longer sticks to the bowl. Cover and leave to rise until doubled in size. Over the first 2 hours, you can make two sets of stretching and folding (see page 89). Then shape the balls, leave them to rest, covered, for 10 minutes, then shape into slightly oblong loaves.

Wait until they have roughly doubled in size and are soft and airy (as far as I'm concerned, this takes about 4 hours at 22°C/71°F). Use your finger to check whether the rise is sufficient.

Shortly before baking, lightly flour and form a roll by pressing with the handle of a spoon. Bake them in an oven with steam preheated to 220°C/425°F/gas 7 for the first 10 minutes, then without steam for 20–25 minutes total until golden brown. Cover them with a cotton cloth while they are still warm so that the crust becomes soft.

 TIP

For bread rolls closer to a traditional bread, you can also use the recipe for Bread in a Flash (page 152).

SOURDOUGH PUMPKIN BREAD

A nice autumnal variation. Pumpkin purée will make this delicious bread even softer and tastier.

LEAVEN:

10 g active starter (2.5%)
40 g strong white (type 812) flour (10%)
40 g water (10%)

Mix the ingredients, cover and wait until doubled in size.

MAIN DOUGH:

200 g baked pumpkin flesh (50%)
350 g strong white (type 812) flour (87.5%)
50 g wholemeal spelt flour (12.5%)
250 g water (62.5%)
8 g salt (2%)

Add 100 g water to the cooked pumpkin flesh and purée in a food processor. Then add the flour and gradually add 120 g of water. Leave to rest, covered, for 30 minutes, then add the leaven and salt. When the dough can absorb a little water again, add the remaining 30 g of water. After a brief rest, knead well two or three times for 2–3 minutes. Over the next 2 hours, make four sets of stretches and folds (see page 89). Leave the dough to rise until doubled in size, then form a large pumpkin shape or several smaller ones. Leave to rise and bake following the instructions on pages 111–114.

TIP

The dough will be a little soft and sticky, which is quite normal. For the pumpkin, bake the pumpkin slices in the oven at 200°C/400°F/gas 6 for about 1 hour, covered for the first 30 minutes, then uncovered. From 400 g of pumpkin slices I got about 200 g of baked pumpkin flesh after baking. You can shape only one large pumpkin or several small ones. In each case, tie the dough after shaping or before baking with twine to get a pumpkin shape. To do this tie four pieces of butcher's string together in the middle, spread them apart, place a loaf in the middle and gently tie over. You can also use this dough for hamburger buns.

GARLIC ROLLS

LEAVEN:

10 g active starter (2%)
20 g strong white (type 812) flour (4%)
20 g wholemeal flour (4%)
30 g water (6%)

Mix the ingredients, cover and wait until doubled in size.

MAIN DOUGH:
(for a 26-cm diameter cake tin)

450 g strong white (type 812) flour (90%)
50 g wholemeal flour (10%)
385 g water (77%)
10 g salt (2%)

COATING:

Melted butter

TOPPING:

6–12 cloves of garlic (optional)
30 g butter, melted
Parsley

Boil 100 g of water, add the 50 g of wholemeal flour and mix well. This allows the flour to absorb the water, making the dough softer. Allow it to cool before adding the remaining flour and gradually adding the remaining water. Leave the dough to rest, covered, for 1 hour, then add the leaven and salt. Knead well. After a brief rest, knead two or three times for 2–3 minutes each. Over the next 2 hours, make four sets of stretches and folds (see page 89).

When the dough has doubled in size, refrigerate overnight. The next day, shape the balls, melt the butter and roll each ball in butter and place in the cake tin. Leave them to rise until doubled in size and airy. Bake with steam in a preheated oven at 200°C/400°F/gas 6 for the first 15 minutes, then uncover and bake until golden brown. Allow them to cool slightly, then brush them with melted butter and scatter with finely chopped garlic and parsley.

SPELT LOAVES WITH CARAMELISED ONIONS

LEAVEN:

10 g active starter (2.5%)
25 g spelt flour (6.2%)
25 g strong white (type 812) flour (6.2%)
40 g water (10%)

Mix the ingredients, cover and wait until doubled in size.

MAIN DOUGH:

200 g spelt flour (50%)
200 g strong white (type 812) flour (50%)
240 g water (6%)
8 g salt (4%)

CARAMELISED ONIONS:
40 g butter (10%)
100 g onions, finely chopped (25%)
1 tablespoon balsamic vinegar

Mix the spelt and strong flour and water until they form a smooth mixture. Leave it to stand, covered, for at least 20 minutes, then add the leaven and salt. Knead well for 4 minutes (first kneading). Leave to rest for 20 minutes.

While the dough is covered, caramelise the finely chopped onions in butter and balsamic vinegar, then drain. Allow the melted fat to cool slightly so that it is not too hot, then add it to the dough. During the second knead, use the slapping and folding technique on the work surface to help the dough absorb the butter. Over the next 2 hours, make five sets of stretches and folds (see page 89) every 20–30 minutes, adding the drained onions to the second set by folding them into the dough. Leave the dough to rise until doubled in size, then shape long loaves according to the instructions on pages 92–96. Dust them with flour and leave to rest, covered, until almost doubled in size again. Before baking, lightly flour them again and score. Bake them with steam in a preheated oven at 240°C/475°F/gas 9 for the first 10 minutes, then without for 15–20 minutes until browned.

TIP You can also use this dough to make delicious baguettes.

HOLIDAY FRUIT BREAD

LEAVEN:

10 g active starter (2%)
25 g strong white (type 812) flour (5%)
25 g rye flour (5%)
40 g water (8%)

Mix the ingredients, cover and wait until doubled in size.

MAIN DOUGH:

150 g rye flour (30%)
250 g strong white (type 812) flour (50%)
100 g white plain (type 550) flour (20%)
325 g water (65%)
10 g salt (2%)

Soaked dried fruit with nuts and dark chocolate
(prepare at least 3-4 days in advance)

Mix all flours and water until they form a smooth mixture. Leave it to stand, covered, for at least 1 hour, then add the leaven and salt. Knead well into dough, then knead two times for 2 minutes. Over 2 hours, make three sets of stretches and folds (see page 89), adding the soaked dried fruits, nuts and dark chocolate to the last set. Knead slowly and gently to blend the ingredients with the dough. Gently knead again after 20 minutes.

During the first 2 hours, you can do two sets of gentle stretches and folds (see page 89). Then leave the dough to rise, covered, for 3–5 hours, until it has risen by about half, then shape it as desired. As the dough will be sticky, roll it in rye flour and leave it to rise in the basket. When it has risen and cracked slightly, it's ready to bake.

Preheat the oven to 240°C/475°F/gas 9, bake for the first 15 minutes, then reduce the temperature to 220°C/425°F/gas 7 and bake for a further 45–50 minutes.

PREPARING THE SOAKED FRUIT WITH NUTS AND DARK CHOCOLATE:

*400 g (80%) dried fruit (i.e. plums, raisins, pears, apples, apricots, figs, dates,
   cranberries), diced*
100 g (20%) roasted nuts (i.e. hazelnuts, walnuts, almonds), chopped
50 g (10%) dark chocolate, finely chopped
90 g rum (20%)
50 g water (10%) or more
Freshly squeezed juice of 2 oranges
Grated zest of 1 organic orange and ½ organic lemon
¼ teaspoon vanilla powder

Mix the fruits, nuts, finely chopped dark chocolate and grated orange and lemon
zest together. Mix the rum, water, and orange juice with the vanilla powder and
pour over the fruit mixture. Leave to soak for at least 3 days, stirring at regular
intervals.

 TIP

You can replace the rum by increasing the volume of freshly squeezed juice and
water. If you are in a hurry, boil the mixture and pour it over the fruit, adding
the chocolate later. Mix several times. Use in the dough the next day. This
bread will keep for a very long time – unless you eat it, of course. It is also a
wonderful gift for Christmas. Everyone here looks forward to receiving them
long in advance.

Sweet and savoury delights

Do not think that sourdough is only suitable for bread: it is absolutely not the case! You can use it for all types of dough for which baker's yeast is usually used. With sourdough, any delicacy becomes even tastier, healthier and more digestible.

The secret of a soft and sweet dough is in the kneading. Before adding the butter, it is essential to knead it well so that it is homogeneous and smooth. After adding the butter at room temperature, carefully knead the dough again so that it absorbs all the fat and becomes soft and silky again. This step usually takes some time. You can use a food processor or knead the dough longer, right on the work surface. This little extra step will be an excellent reason to eat it afterwards without feeling any remorse.

BURGER BUNS

SWEET STIFF STARTER:

140 g sweet stiff starter (28%) (see page 63)

Preparation takes about a day and a half (at 21°C/69°F). Mix 10 g of active starter with 30 g strong white (type 812) flour, 10 g water and 8 g soft brown sugar. Leave until the starter has doubled in size. Then feed it again with 50 g strong white (type 812) flour, 20 g water and 12 g soft brown sugar. When it has tripled in size, add the starter to the dough.

MAIN DOUGH:
(for about a dozen buns)

400 g white plain (type 550) flour (80%)
100 g strong white (type 812) flour (20%)
2 eggs (108 g, 22%)
190 g milk (38%)
8 g salt (1.6%)
10 g sugar (2%)
80 g butter, at room temperature (16%)

EGG GLAZE:

1 egg
1 tablespoon milk
Pinch of salt

Sift the flours into a mixer bowl. Tear the sweet stiff starter into small pieces. Mix all the remaining dough ingredients together except the butter, then add the sweet stiff starter to this liquid to dissolve it. Start the food processor at the lowest speed and slowly pour the liquid mixture into the bowl. Knead until the dough comes away from the bowl, then gradually add the butter in pieces. Increase the speed and knead until the dough is soft and smooth. If you do not have a food processor, you can slap and fold the dough on the work surface as described on page 86. Leave the dough to rise in a closed container, stretching and folding it two times during the first hour (see page 89).

For the egg glaze mix all the ingredients together to form a runny/smooth glaze.

Leave the dough to rise covered until doubled in size, then shape into balls, brush them with the egg glaze and cover with cling film. Leave to rise covered until doubled in size and puffy. At 21°C/69°F, they will rise in 4–5 hours. Preheat the oven to 200°C/400°F/gas 6, brush the rolls with the egg glaze again, scatter with sesame or poppy seeds and bake for 20–30 minutes until golden brown.

 TIP

Brush the still warm breads with butter to obtain a nice soft crust. These buns are also perfect for burgers. They are soft enough but not too compact.

SAVOURY PLAIT

SWEET STIFF STARTER:

140 g sweet stiff starter (28%) (see page 63)

The preparation takes about a day and a half (at a temperature of 21°C/69°F). Mix 10 g of active starter with 30 g strong white (type 812) flour, 10 g water and 8 g soft brown sugar. Leave to rest until the starter has doubled in size. Then feed it again with another 50 g strong white (type 812) flour, 20 g water and 12 g soft brown sugar. When it has tripled in size, use the starter in the dough.

MAIN DOUGH:
(for one large 35-cm plait, two medium plaits or four smaller ones)

400 g white plain (type 550) flour (80%)
100 g strong white (type 812) flour (20%)
2 eggs (108 g, 22%)
100 g milk (25%)
90 g water (18%)
8 g salt (1.6%)
10 g sugar (2%)
50 g butter, at room temperature (10%)

EGG GLAZE:

1 egg
1 tablespoon milk
Pinch of salt

FOR THE TOPPING

Sesame seeds, poppy seeds, flaked almonds (optional)

Sift the flours into a mixer bowl. Tear the sweet stiff starter into small pieces. Mix all the remaining dough ingredients together except the butter, then add the sweet stiff starter to this liquid to dissolve it. Start the food processor at the lowest speed and slowly pour the liquid mixture into the bowl. Knead until the dough comes away from the bowl, then gradually add the butter in pieces. Increase the speed and knead until the dough is soft and smooth. Place the dough in a bowl and cover it, make two sets of stretches and folds in the first hour (see page 89), then leave it to rise until it has doubled in size. Shape into three lengths and weave them into a plait.

For the egg glaze mix all the ingredients together to form a runny/smooth glaze.

Brush the plait with the egg glaze, cover with cling film and leave to rise until it has doubled in volume and is very soft. At 21°C/69°F, the plait will rise in 3–5 hours. Before baking, brush with the egg glaze again, scatter with sesame or poppy seeds as desired and bake in a preheated oven at 200°C/400°F/gas 6 for 30–40 minutes until golden brown.

 TIP

If the eggs are small, make up the difference with milk. You can also use this dough for milk bread.

SWEET PLAIT

SWEET STIFF STARTER:

140 g sweet stiff starter (28%) (see page 63)

The preparation takes about a day and a half (at a temperature of 21°C/69°F). Mix 10 g active starter with 30 g strong white (type 812) flour, 10 g water and 8 g soft brown sugar. Leave to rest until the leaven has doubled in size. Then feed it again with another 50 g strong white (type 812) flour, 20 g water and 12 g soft brown sugar. When it has tripled in size, use the starter in the dough.

MAIN DOUGH:

500 g white plain (type 550) flour (100%)
2 eggs (108 g, 22%)
180 g milk (36%)
Grated zest of 1 organic lemon and juice of ½ lemon
30 g soft brown sugar (6%)
8 g salt (1.6%)
20 g rum (4%)
60 g butter, at room temperature (12%)

EGG GLAZE:

1 egg
1 tablespoon milk
Pinch of salt

Sift the flours into a mixer bowl. Tear the sweet stiff starter into small pieces. Mix all the remaining dough ingredients together except the butter, then add the sweet stiff starter to this liquid to dissolve it. Start the food processor at the lowest speed and slowly pour the liquid mixture into the bowl. Knead until the dough comes away from the bowl, then gradually add the butter in pieces. Increase the speed and knead until the dough is soft and smooth. Place the dough in a bowl and cover it, make two sets of stretches and folds in the first hour (see page 89), then leave it to rise until it has doubled in size. Shape into three strands and weave them into a plait.

For the egg glaze mix all the ingredients together to form a runny/smooth glaze.

Brush the plait with the egg glaze, cover with cling film and leave to rise until it has doubled in volume and is very soft. At 21°C/69°F, the plait will rise in 3–5 hours. Before baking, brush with the egg glaze again and bake in a preheated oven at 200°C/400°F/gas 6 for about 30 minutes until golden brown.

 TIP

For a festive touch, you can add raisins soaked in rum or fruit juice to the dough.

WALNUT ROLL

Walnut roll or the so-called *potica* pronounced 'potitza' is the most traditional Slovenian sweet leavened treat; there's no feast without it.

The most typical filling is this walnut one but there are many different types of fillings, as for example poppy seed, tarragon and cottage cheese (sweet), chocolate, and many more.

SWEET STIFF STARTER:

105 g sweet stiff starter (24%) (see page 63)

The preparation takes about a day and a half (at a temperature of 21°C/69°F). Mix 5 g active starter with 25 g strong white (type 812) flour, 10 g water and 5 g soft brown sugar. Leave to rest until the starter has doubled in size. Then feed it again with another 35 g strong white (type 812) flour, 15 g water and 10 g soft brown sugar. When it has tripled in size, use the starter in the dough.

MAIN DOUGH:
(for a 30-cm diameter cake tin)

450 g white plain (type 550) flour (100%)
3 egg yolks (60 g, 13%)
170 g milk (38%)
20 g rum (44%)
60 g soft brown sugar (13%)
7 g salt (1.5%)
1 tablespoon lemon juice
Grated zest of 1 organic lemon
60 g butter, at room temperature (13%)

WALNUT FILLING:

500 g ground walnuts
40 g rum
1 egg
3 egg whites, beaten (leftover from the dough)
50 g soft brown sugar
100 g milk (or more if necessary – the filling should be spreadable)

EGG GLAZE:

1 egg
1 tablespoon cream
pinch of salt

Sift the flour into a mixer bowl. Tear the sweet stiff starter into small pieces. Mix all the remaining dough ingredients together except the butter, then add the sweet stiff starter to this liquid to dissolve it. Start the food processor at the lowest speed and slowly pour the liquid mixture into the bowl. Knead until the dough comes away from the bowl, then gradually add the butter in pieces. Increase the speed and knead until the dough is soft and smooth. Place the dough in a bowl and cover it, make two sets of stretches and folds in the first hour (see page 89), then leave it to rise until it has doubled in size.

To make the walnut filling mix all the ingredients together, add milk gradually. In case the filling is too stiff, add some more milk. If it's too soft, add more walnuts. It needs to be spreadable.

For the egg glaze mix all the ingredients together to form a runny/smooth glaze.

If stored in the refrigerator, bring the dough back to room temperature and leave to rise before the next step. Roll it into a square about 8 mm thick, then spread the walnut filling over it and roll tightly like a Swiss roll. Put the dough into a greased cake tin. Leave it to rise covered until doubled in size. I find it takes almost 8–10 hours, due to the weight of the filling. Before baking, brush with the egg glaze. Bake in a preheated oven at 190°C/375°F/gas 5, covered, for the first 20 minutes, then lower the heat to 180°C/350°F/gas 4 and bake for about 1 hour until brown. After baking, leave it in the tin for about 15 minutes, then transfer it to the wire rack.

 TIP

If the dough shrinks when you roll it, leave it, covered, for about 20 minutes. Afterwards, you should then be able to roll it easily.

BUTTER BRIOCHE

SWEET STIFF STARTER:

245 g sweet stiff starter (49%) (see page 63)

The preparation takes about a day and a half (at a temperature of 21°C/69°F). Mix 10 g active starter with 50 g strong white (type 812) flour, 20 g water and 12 g soft brown sugar. Leave to rest until the starter has doubled in size. Then feed it again with another 90 g strong white (type 812) flour, 40 g water and 23 g soft brown sugar. When it has tripled in size, use the starter in the dough.

MAIN DOUGH:

500 g white plain (type 550) flour (100%)
75 g soft brown sugar (15%)
175 g eggs (35%)
7.5 g salt (1.5%)
60 g cream (12%)
2.5 g vanilla powder or 8 g organic vanilla sugar (0.05%)
125 g butter, room temperature (25%)

EGG GLAZE:

1 egg
1 tablespoon cream
Pinch of salt

Sift the flour into a mixer bowl. Tear the sweet stiff starter into small pieces. Mix all the remaining dough ingredients together except the butter, then add the sweet stiff starter to this liquid to dissolve it. Start the food processor at the lowest speed and slowly pour the liquid mixture into the bowl. The dough will be very compact.

Knead until the dough comes away from the bowl, then increase the speed and gradually add the butter in pieces. Knead until you have a soft and smooth dough. I do this next step on the work surface, adding the butter in four or five steps. Put the dough into a bowl, cover and leave to rise until doubled in size.

It can be refrigerated overnight. If stored in the refrigerator, bring it back to room temperature and leave to rise before the next step.

For the egg glaze mix all the ingredients together to form a runny/smooth glaze.

Roll the dough out into a sausage shape and place in a greased baking tin. Brush it with the egg glaze, cover with cling film and leave it to rise until doubled in size. Bake in a preheated oven at 190°C/375°F/gas 5 until it has a nice yellow colour, then lower the temperature to 170°C/340°F/gas 3½ and bake until nicely browned.

 TIP

The dough will be very firm before adding the butter, but when you add the butter it will gradually become softer.

CHOCOLATE BABKA

Butter brioche dough from the previous page

FILLING:

200 g dark chocolate
100 g butter
Pinch of salt
¼ teaspoon vanilla powder or 8 g vanilla sugar
200 g ground hazelnuts

EGG GLAZE:

1 egg
1 tablespoon cream
Pinch of salt

Prepare the filling: melt the chocolate and butter, then add the salt, vanilla and sugar to taste and ground hazelnuts. As far as I'm concerned, I don't add sugar as the chocolate is already sweet enough. Mix thoroughly. If the filling is too thin, refrigerate for about 30 minutes to make it easier to spread. After the first rising, roll out the butter brioche dough into a square about 5 mm thick, cover with the filling, roll up into a sausage shape and cut in half lengthways. Twist and join the ends in a circle. The result will be a delicious chocolate and nut babka.

For the egg glaze mix all the ingredients together to form a runny/smooth glaze.

Place the dough on a sheet of baking paper, brush with the egg glaze, cover with cling film and leave to rise until doubled in size. Brush again with the egg glaze. Bake in a preheated oven at 190°C/375°F/gas 5 until the babka has a nice yellow colour. Then lower the temperature to 170°C/340°F/gas 3½ and continue cooking until golden brown.

TIP

Instead of the chocolate hazelnut filling, you can also use a thick jam. A home-made plum jam goes wonderfully with the buttery crumb. Or you can replace the hazelnuts with ground walnuts, almonds, etc. If you find the brioche dough is too heavy, you can try the sweet plait dough on page 204 for a lighter version.

BRIOCHE BUNS WITH JAM

SWEET STIFF STARTER:

140 g sweet stiff starter (28%) (see page 63)

The preparation takes about a day and a half (at a temperature of 21°C/69°F). Mix 10 g active starter with 30 g strong white (type 812) flour, 10 g water and 10 g soft brown sugar. Leave to rest until the starter has doubled in size. Then feed it again with another 50 g strong white (type 812) flour, 20 g water and 12 g soft brown sugar. When it has tripled in size, use the starter in the dough.

MAIN DOUGH:

500 g white plain (type 550) flour (100%)
2 eggs (108 g, 22%)
180 g milk (36%)
Grated zest of 1 organic lemon and juice of ½ lemon
30 g soft brown sugar (6%)
8 g salt (1.6%)
20 g rum (4%)
60 g butter, at room temperature (12%)

FILLING:

A stiff jam of your choice, such as plum

EGG GLAZE:

1 egg
1 tablespoon cream
Pinch of salt

Sift the flour into a mixer bowl. Tear the sweet stiff starter into small pieces. Mix all the remaining dough ingredients together except the butter, then add the sweet stiff starter to this liquid to dissolve it. Start the food processor at the lowest speed and slowly pour the liquid mixture into the bowl. Knead until the dough comes away from the bowl, then gradually add the butter in pieces.

Increase the speed and knead until the dough is soft and smooth. Place the dough in a bowl covered, make two sets of stretches and folds in the first hour (see page 89), then leave it to rise until it has doubled in size.

The dough can be refrigerated overnight. If stored in the refrigerator, bring the dough back to room temperature and leave to rise before the next step.

For the egg glaze mix all the ingredients together to form a runny/smooth glaze.

Divide the dough into round rolls, add the desired amount of jam or other filling, seal and shape into balls. Place in a greased dish. Brush with the egg glaze, cover with cling film and leave to rise until they have doubled in size and risen well. Brush again with the egg glaze. Bake in an oven preheated to 190°C/375°F/gas 5 until they turn yellow, then lower the temperature to 170°C/340°F/gas 3½ and bake until golden brown.

 TIP

For even softer buns, brush them evenly with butter while they are still warm. The rum can be replaced with orange juice.

BERLINER DOUGHNUTS

These sourdough doughnuts can be made any time of the year. They taste, to put it simply, extraordinarily delicious.

SWEET STIFF STARTER:

245 g sweet stiff starter (61%) (see page 63)

The preparation takes about a day and a half (at a temperature of 21°C/69°F). Mix 10 g active starter with 50 g strong white (type 812) flour, 20 g water and 12 g soft brown sugar. Leave to rest until the starter has doubled in size. Then feed it again with another 90 g strong white (type 812) flour, 40 g water and 23 g soft brown sugar. When it has tripled in size, use the starter in the dough.

MAIN DOUGH:
(for about 14 doughnuts, 65 g each)

400 g white plain (type 550) flour (100%)
4 egg yolks (80 g, 20%)
150 g milk (37%)
30 g rum (7.5%)
35 g soft brown sugar (9%)
½ teaspoon vanilla powder
6 g salt (1.5%)
Grated zest of 1 lemon
40 g butter, at room temperature (10%)

FOR FRYING:

Vegetable oil

Sift the flour into a mixer bowl. Tear the sweet stiff starter into small pieces. Mix all the remaining dough ingredients together except the butter, then add the sweet stiff starter to this liquid to dissolve it. Start the food processor at the lowest speed and slowly pour the liquid mixture into the bowl. Knead until the dough comes away from the bowl, then gradually add the butter in pieces.

Put the dough into a container and store it, covered, in the refrigerator overnight. The next day, bring the dough to room temperature and leave it to rise until doubled in size. Then weigh out 14 pieces of dough about 65 g each and shape them into balls (see page 126). Place them on a lightly floured cloth, press them gently flat, cover with cling film and leave them to rise until doubled in size and soft. At home, it usually takes 7–8 hours at 21–22°C/69–71°F.

Add oil to a casserole to at least 3.5 cm of depth and slowly heat it to 165–170°C/325–340°F/gas mark 3–3½. Place the doughnuts in the oil with the side that was resting on the cloth facing up. Cover the dish with a lid and fry the doughnuts for 3–4 minutes on one side, then remove the lid, turn the doughnuts over and fry for a further 3–4 minutes.

 TIP

Fill the still hot doughnuts with your favourite jam or other filling. It will be easier to use the jam for filling if you heat it slightly.

DANISH PASTRIES

SWEET STIFF STARTER:

100 g sweet stiff starter (20%) (see page 63)

The preparation takes about a day and a half (at a temperature of 21°C/69°F). Mix 5 g active starter with 25 g strong white (type 812) flour, 10 g water and 5 g soft brown sugar. Leave to rest until the starter has doubled in size. Then feed it again with another 35 g strong white (type 812) flour, 10 g water and 10 g soft brown sugar. When it has tripled in size, use the starter in the dough.

MAIN DOUGH:

500 g white plain (type 550) flour (100%)
250 g cold water (50%)
30 g powdered milk (6%)
20 g soft brown sugar (4%)
8 g salt (1.6%)
320 g butter, for folding (64%)

EGG GLAZE:

1 egg
1 tablespoon milk
Pinch of salt

CURD FILLING:

200 g curd or fromage frais, drained
1 egg
Sugar to taste
Fruit of choice

Sift the flour into a mixer bowl. Tear the sweet stiff starter into small pieces. Mix all the remaining dough ingredients together except the butter, then add the sweet stiff starter to this liquid to dissolve it. Start the food processor at the lowest speed and slowly pour the liquid mixture into the bowl. Knead until the dough comes away from the bowl. Increase the speed and knead until the dough is soft and smooth. Refrigerate in a sealed container for 8 hours or overnight. The next day, leave the dough at room temperature (21°C/69°F) for about 45 minutes. Meanwhile, roll out a 20-cm square of butter.

The dough and butter square should be at about the same temperature. The butter should be kneadable but not too soft, otherwise put it into the freezer for 5 minutes.

Roll the dough into a roughly 30 x 30-cm square so it is large enough to enclose the butter. Seal the dough around the butter well so it does not leak. Make three sets of letter folds. After each fold, wrap the dough in cling film and refrigerate for 30 minutes. After the last fold, wrap the dough again in cling film and refrigerate until the next day.

The next day, leave the dough to stand at room temperature for 40–50 minutes, then roll it into a 4-mm thick rectangle. Trim the edges, cut into squares and make into different shapes. Place them on a baking tray lined with baking paper and brush with the egg glaze. Cover them with cling film and leave them to rise until doubled in size at room temperature (21°C/69°F for 8–10 hours).

When they have sufficiently risen and are light and puffy, fill them with the curd filling and fruit. Brush them again with the egg glaze and bake in a preheated oven at 220°C/425°F/gas 7 for 5 minutes, then lower the temperature to 190°C/375°F/gas 5 and bake until they are browned.

The folding and shaping process is explained on pages 130–138.

 TIP

You can make different shapes from this dough. You can also fill it with the curd filling, then roll the dough into smaller rolls and slice. Try scattering the dough with a mixture of cinnamon, sugar and raisins, then roll and slice.

CROISSANTS

SWEET STIFF STARTER:

140 g sweet stiff starter (28%) (see page 63)

The preparation takes about a day and a half (at a temperature of 21°C/69°F). Mix 10 g active starter with 30 g manitoba flour, 10 g water and 8 g soft brown sugar. Leave to rest until the starter has doubled in size. Then feed it again with another 50 g manitoba flour, 20 g water and 12 g soft brown sugar. When it has tripled in size, use the starter in the dough.

MAIN DOUGH:

500 g manitoba wheat flour (100%)
210 g cold milk (42%)
80 g water (16%)
20 g soft brown sugar (4%)
9 g salt (1.8%)

300 g butter for folding (60%)

EGG GLAZE:

1 egg
1½ teaspoons fresh cream
Pinch of salt

Reserve the butter for the next day. Dissolve the salt, sugar and sweet stiff starter in milk and water, sift the flour into a mixer bowl and then slowly pour in the liquid ingredients. Knead it on the second setting for 7–10 minutes to obtain a dense, smooth dough. Refrigerate in a sealed container for 8 hours or overnight.

The next day, bring the dough to room temperature for about 45 minutes (21°C/69°F). Meanwhile, roll out the butter to a 20-cm square. The dough and butter square should be at about the same temperature. The butter should be pliable but not too soft, otherwise put it into the freezer for 5 minutes. Roll the dough into a roughly 30 x 30-cm square so that it is large enough to enclose the butter.

Seal the dough well around the butter so that it does not leak. Make three sets of letter folds or one set of book folds (see pages 132-135). After each fold, wrap the dough in cling film and refrigerate for 30 minutes. After the last fold, wrap the dough again in cling film and refrigerate until the next day. The next morning, leave the dough to stand at room temperature for 40–50 minutes, then roll it into a 4-mm thick rectangle, cut into triangles and roll into croissants.

For the egg glaze mix all the ingredients together to form a runny/smooth glaze.

Brush the croissants with the egg glaze and place them on a baking tray, cover them with cling film and leave to rise at room temperature until they have doubled in size (21°C/69°F for 8–10 hours). When sufficiently risen, they will be soft and puffy. Brush them again with the egg glaze and bake in a preheated oven at 220°C/425°F/gas 7 for 5 minutes, then lower the temperature to 190°C/375°F/gas 5 and bake until they are nicely brown.

The folding and shaping process is explained on pages 130-136.

TIP

Choose a day when the room temperature is not too high: 20–21°C/68-69°F will be best. Don't worry if you fail to make croissants on your first attempt – it usually takes at least three or four tries. You can put the rolling pin in the refrigerator for at least 1 hour before use.

HOT CROSS BUNS

SWEET STIFF STARTER:

140 g sweet stiff starter (35%) (see page 63)

The preparation takes about a day and a half (at a temperature of 21°C/69°F). Mix 10 g active starter with 30 g strong white (type 812) flour, 10 g water and 8 g soft brown sugar. Leave to rest until the starter has doubled in size. Then feed it again with another 50 g strong white (type 812) flour, 20 g water and 12 g soft brown sugar. When it has tripled in size, use the starter in the dough.

MAIN DOUGH:
(for a round 26-cm baking tin)

400 g white plain (type 550) flour (100%)
200 g milk (50%)
20 g powdered milk (6%, if desired)
30 g soft brown sugar (4%)
1 egg (54 g, 1.4%)
6 g salt (1.5%)
Juice of ½ orange
Grazed zest of ½ organic orange and ½ organic lemon
½ teaspoon ground cinnamon
½ teaspoon ground cloves
½ teaspoon ground cardamom
½ teaspoon ground ginger
½ teaspoon ground nutmeg
40 g butter, at room temperature (10%)
2 pinches of vanilla powder
140 g raisins (soaked in rum for at least 7 hours) (35%)

EGG GLAZE:

1 egg
1 tablespoon milk
Pinch of salt

WHITE LINES:

White flour and water (the dough should be fluid enough to draw with it but not so much as to be runny)

Sift the flour into a mixer bowl. Tear the sweet stiff starter into small pieces. Mix all the remaining dough ingredients together except the butter, then add the sweet stiff starter to this liquid to dissolve it. Start the food processor at the lowest speed and slowly pour the liquid mixture into the bowl. Knead until the dough comes away from the bowl, then gradually add the butter in pieces. Increase the speed and knead until you have a soft smooth dough.

For the egg glaze mix all the ingredients together to form a runny/smooth glaze.

Slowly add drained raisins – you can do this by hand. Fold the dough into an oiled container with a lid and make two sets of stretches and folds in the first hour (see page 89). When it has risen and doubled in size, shape the dough into balls and place them in a greased baking tin. Cover them with cling film and leave to rise until almost doubled in size, then coat with the egg glaze. Prepare the white line mixture (adjust the density to your flour as needed).

Using a syringe, draw crosses over the buns and bake them in a preheated oven at 220°C/425°F/gas 7 for 10 minutes, then lower the temperature to 200°C/400°F/gas 6 and bake until the buns are golden brown.

 TIP

If you brush the buns with butter after baking, the crust will become nicely soft.

SEMOLINA CHEESECAKE

Savoury or sweet, this bake is always a pleasure!

SWEET STIFF STARTER:

100 g sweet stiff starter (25%) (see page 63)

The preparation takes about a day and a half (at a temperature of 21°C/69°F). Mix 5 g active starter with 20 g strong white (type 812) flour, 5 g water and 5 g soft brown sugar. Leave to rest until the starter has doubled in size. Then feed it again with another 40 g strong white (type 812) flour, 15 g water and 10 g soft brown sugar. When it has tripled in size, use the starter in the dough.

MAIN DOUGH:

200 g fine wheat flour (50%)
200 g regular white plain (type 550) flour (50%)
200 g milk (50%)
1 egg (54 g, 14%)
8 g salt (2%)
20 g butter, at room temperature (10%)

FILLING:

70 g boiling water
70 g wheat semolina
800 g cottage cheese
2 eggs (about 106 g)
200 g sour cream
100 g soft brown sugar
2 pinches of salt

COATING:

150 g sour cream
1 egg
Pinch of salt
Sugar, to taste (I usually add a tablespoon of soft brown sugar)

EGG GLAZE:

1 egg
1 tablespoon milk
Pinch of salt

Sift the flour into a mixer bowl. Tear the sweet stiff starter into small pieces. Mix all the remaining dough ingredients together except the butter, then add the sweet stiff starter to this liquid to dissolve it. Start the food processor at the lowest speed and slowly pour the liquid mixture into the bowl. Knead until the dough comes away from the bowl, then gradually add the butter in pieces. Increase the speed and knead until you have a soft smooth dough.

Put the dough into a bowl covered and make two sets of stretches and folds in the first hour (see page 89). Then store it, covered, overnight – it can be refrigerated but it is not necessary. Leave the dough to rise until doubled in size.

In the meantime, prepare the filling. Pour boiling water over the semolina and allow it to cool slightly. Drain the cheese and mix it with the eggs, sour cream, salt, sugar and boiled semolina. Then roll out the dough to about 1.5 cm thick and place it on a greased, large round or rectangular baking tray.

For the egg glaze mix all the ingredients together to form a runny/smooth glaze.

Roll the edges of the dough up and spread the filling over the dough. Brush the dough with the egg glaze, cover with cling film and leave to rise until doubled in size. Mix all the ingredients for the coating together and pour over the filling immediately before baking. Bake in a preheated oven at 180–200°C/350–400°F/gas 4–6 for 1 hour.

VEGAN BANANA BREAD

(for a 20 x 10.5 x 7-cm loaf tin)

2 very ripe bananas (about 145 g)

100 g melted coconut oil
8 g organic vanilla sugar or ¼ teaspoon vanilla powder
½ teaspoon of cinnamon
50 g soft brown sugar
2 pinches of salt
200 g active starter
250 g white or wholemeal spelt flour

Mash the bananas with a fork, add the melted coconut oil, vanilla sugar, cinnamon, soft brown sugar and salt. You can also add all these ingredients to a blender. Then add the starter and mix well. Sift the flour into a bowl and slowly pour in the liquid mixture. Knead into a soft and smooth dough. Roll up into a sausage shape.

Grease the loaf tin and place the dough in it, cover and leave to rise until doubled in size. Bake in a preheated oven at 180–190°C/350–375°F/gas 4–5 for 40–50 minutes or until a skewer inserted into the centre comes out clean. After the cake is baked, brush it with warm coconut oil and place on a wire rack to cool.

TIP

You can substitute coconut oil with regular melted butter.

SPELT FRUITCAKE

My favourite cake, juicy, delicious and moist.

LEAVEN:

200 g active starter
200 g white or wholemeal spelt flour
About 200 g milk (adapt to the flour – this leaven should be thick)

Mix the ingredients, cover and wait until doubled in size.

MAIN DOUGH:
(for a round 26-cm diameter baking tin)

2 eggs
200 g melted butter
120 g soft brown sugar
½ teaspoon vanilla powder
½ teaspoon bicarbonate of soda
Pinch of salt
30 g cocoa powder

FILLING:

*200 g of frozen or fresh fruit (sour cherries, raspberries, plums, peaches, blueberries)
scattered with spelt flour*

Mix the eggs, melted butter, soft brown sugar, vanilla, bicarbonate of soda, salt
and cocoa well, then add the leaven. Pour the mixture into a greased baking tin
and top with the fruit. Bake the cake in a preheated oven at 180–190°C/350–
375°F/gas 4–5 for about 50 minutes, until a skewer inserted into the centre
comes out clean.

TIP

For a vegan version, replace the milk with coconut milk, and add 2 tablespoons
of ground linseed (flaxseed) and 10 g of melted coconut oil in place of the eggs.

What if there's too much starter?

Sometimes the starter just keeps multiplying. So in this chapter, I've put together some ideas on what to do when you have an abundance of sourdough starter and don't want to make bread, or you simply want to try using it to improve the taste of other foods. How you use the starter depends exclusively on you and your imagination.

KHORASAN BISCUITS

(for a 44 x 39-cm baking tray)

300 g khorasan white flour
100 g butter
1 egg, beaten
50 g active starter
Pinch of salt
80 g soft brown sugar
8 g organic vanilla sugar or ¼ teaspoon vanilla powder
2 tablespoons water (if needed)

Sift the flour into the bowl and mix the cold butter into it, then add the beaten egg with the active starter, salt, soft brown sugar and vanilla sugar. Knead and add a tablespoon of water at a time as needed. Leave to stand, covered, at room temperature for 4 hours, then refrigerate overnight. The next day, bring the dough back to room temperature for 1–2 hours. Then roll it between two sheets of baking paper and cut it or cut out the shapes with a biscuit cutter. Bake in a preheated oven at 200°C/400°F/gas 6 until the edges turn brown.

TIP

Spices of your choice – cinnamon, cardamom, ginger – can be added to the biscuits to enhance the flavour. You can also use another flour such as white plain or strong flour. The dough is also suitable for making jam-filled Linzer cookies.

SOURDOUGH PANCAKES

75 g active starter
130 g strong white (type 812) flour
300 g milk
4 g salt

Use a whisk to combine all the ingredients, except the salt, until completely mixed and smooth, then leave to stand, covered, until numerous bubbles form on the surface and the mixture rises slightly. You can also refrigerate it overnight, or at least for 3–5 hours. Then add the salt. If desired, you can dilute the mixture with milk to the desired consistency or add an egg and whisk well to make the pancakes denser. Cook them in a frying pan in coconut oil, olive oil or butter. These pancakes are very light and airy.

TIP

A plant-based milk is a perfect substitute for cow's milk for vegan pancakes. By replacing half of the flour with spelt or khorasan flour, the pancakes will be even tastier. For sweet pancakes, add sugar to taste to the basic recipe.

SHREDDED PANCAKES

3 heaped tablespoons of active starter (about 60 g)
300 g milk
2 pinches of salt
250 g flour (e.g. strong white/type 812 flour)
3 eggs
¼ teaspoon vanilla powder or 8 g organic vanilla sugar
1 tablespoon coconut sugar

Butter and coconut sugar for caramelising

Mix all the ingredients together and leave until the mixture starts to bubble (even overnight or refrigerated). Then mix gently and pour into a hot greased frying pan until about 1 cm thick. Cover and cook over medium heat for 5–10 minutes, then turn it over and cook on the other side. Take this thick pancake out of the pan and cut it into pieces – a bench knife will be useful for this. Melt 2 tablespoons of butter in a pan, add a level tablespoon of coconut sugar, caramelise nicely, add the pancake slices and mix well. Serve hot, but these slices are also delicious cold.

TIP

You can replace half of the flour with wholemeal flour. A combination of half khorasan flour and half white plain flour is also excellent. If you don't have coconut sugar, use brown sugar.

SHORTCRUST PASTRY CASE

(for a 26-cm diameter tart tin)

170 g active starter
250 g white or wholemeal spelt flour (or half of each)
40 g soft brown sugar
Pinch of salt
200 g cold butter

Mix the flour and starter in a food processor fitted with a knife blade. Add the sugar, a pinch of salt and then gradually add the 200 g of cold butter. Roll out the dough and line the tart tin. Cover it with cling film and refrigerate overnight, then prick the dough and bake blind in a preheated oven at 180°C/350°F/gas 4 for 15–20 minutes. Add the filling and bake until done.

 TIP

If you do not have a food processor, start by mixing the starter and flour into a rough mixture. Then add the rest of the ingredients and knead the dough as quickly as possible.

BATTER FOR FRYING

100 g active starter
50 g milk or water
50 g white plain (types 405 or 550) or strong white (type 812) flour
1 egg
salt and pepper to taste

Mix all the ingredients together to make a fairly thick, but still runny batter. Leave to stand, covered, for 3–4 hours or overnight in the refrigerator. The batter should be bubbly. First dry the food you want to fry, then dip it into the batter.

TIP

If you omit the egg and use water, this batter will also be suitable for vegans. It is excellent mixed with chilli powder.

GRATED DUMPLINGS

350 g flour
150 g active starter
1 egg

Knead all the ingredients, adding more flour if necessary, then leave the dough to rest in the refrigerator for about 3 hours or overnight. The dough can be kneaded again before grating. Cook the grated dough in boiling salted water or dry it for later use. Excellent in soup.

WHOLEGRAIN CRACKERS

(for a 44 x 39-cm baking tray)

200 g wholemeal flour
90 g active starter
5 g salt
100 g butter, at room temperature
10–20 g water

Mix the flour, starter and salt into a rough crumbly mixture by hand. Add the butter in pieces to the mixture and knead. If the dough becomes too firm, add a little more water. The dough should be dense but kneadable. Leave to stand, covered, for at least 3–5 hours or refrigerate overnight. If stored in the refrigerator, the dough should return to room temperature before being worked.

Roll out the dough between two sheets of baking paper to 2–3 mm thick, cut to size and prick with a fork. Scatter with your choice of sesame seeds, poppy seeds or coarse salt and bake in a preheated oven at 200°C/400°F/gas 6 for 15–20 minutes until golden brown.

TIP

You can also use wholemeal spelt flour or some other type of flour instead of wholemeal wheat flour. Brush the crackers with a beaten egg before scattering the toppings over them.

SPELT BREADSTICKS

For two or three 44 x 39-cm baking trays:

200 g wholemeal spelt flour
200 g white spelt flour
215 g water
80 g active starter
20 g olive oil
8 g salt

Mix the flours and water until a fairly dense dough. Leave it to stand, covered, for at least 20 minutes, then add the starter, oil and salt. Knead firmly so that all ingredients are well incorporated. During the next 2 hours, the dough can be stretched and folded four times (see page 89), but this is not necessary.

Leave the dough until doubled in size, then turn out onto a well-floured work surface, fold over, scatter with plenty of flour and cut into strips with the bench knife. Shape these strips into balls, then roll them by hand into thin sticks before being floured. Place on baking paper, cover and leave to rest for 1–2 hours. Bake in an oven with steam preheated to 190°C/375°F/gas 5 for 10 minutes, then without steam for 10–20 minutes. Cooking time depends on the diameter of the sticks.

 TIP

You can also use wheat flour. While kneading, you can add rosemary, sesame seeds or other seeds to the dough.

Anita Šumer

— The quest for —

SOURDOUGH

FRESH SOURDOUGH PASTA

Sourdough is perfectly suited to making pasta, which will be even easier to digest and softer.

180 g strong white (type 812) flour
20 g einkorn flour
160 g active starter
40 g water

Knead all the ingredients together. When kneading the dough, it should be very dense but still easily kneaded as it will soften later during the fermentation process. Leave to rest for at least 3–4 hours at room temperature. Then knead the dough well and roll it out on a well-floured work surface or using a pasta machine.

I rolled the pieces of dough myself on the 3/9 setting and then on the 6/9 setting. Cut the strips to the desired size and cook them in salted boiling water. Note that this pasta cooks very quickly to al dente and barely a minute is enough! If all the fresh dough is not used, it is better to freeze it quickly rather than dry it, as the microorganisms can break down the dough further when at room temperature and the dough may disintegrate.

 TIP

You can use any flour to your liking, but you will need to adjust the amount of water.

SOAKING SEEDS, NUTS AND WHOLEGRAINS WITH SOURDOUGH

If you soak seeds, nuts or wholegrains overnight to use when making bread products, you can also add a teaspoon of starter to the water – your body will be grateful.

PICKLED TURNIP WITH SOURDOUGH

At a workshop, Jasna, a participant, told me that she had read in an article by Danica Petrovič how turnip is fermented in the Haloze region of Slovenia: you put a little starter in a pot, grate the turnip on top and pour water over it. The jar is placed in a warm place, near an oven for example, and the pickled turnip is ready in 3–4 days. The particularity of this type of preparation is also the fact that milk diluted with a little water does not curdle when this turnip is boiled. Of course, I wanted to try it. I peeled the turnip, cut it and prepared it as mentioned. I covered the container and weighted down the turnip. After 4 days, I was able to enjoy some fantastic pickled turnip. I can easily imagine that sourdough is also suitable for other vegetables.

SOURDOUGH AS A BINDER

You can also add starter to your favourite recipes for patties, meatballs, various other fillings (such as stuffed peppers), etc. This will further enhance the taste.

THICKENER FOR SOUPS AND SAUCES

To thicken soups or sauces, simply dissolve a tablespoon of sourdough starter in a little water and stir. Cook the soup or sauce until it thickens. Its thickness will depend on the quantity of the starter. For my part, I add 1–2 tablespoons of starter to a litre of soup.

FILO PASTRY FOR STRUDEL

Sourdough can also be used to prepare a strudel pastry without adding acid or lemon juice, as the lactic acid bacteria ensure the dough's elasticity.

filo pastry for strudel:

30 g bubbly, active starter
150 g water (or more if needed)
6 g salt
300 g white plain flour

Mix the starter with the water and salt, pour the mixture gradually into the flour, then mix it all together. Knead until smooth and cover for a good hour at room temperature. Then place the dough in the refrigerator for at least 12 hours. The dough must not rise. If this happens, simply knead it and leave it to rest for at least 20 minutes. Wait until the dough is at room temperature before stretching it. Top it with your favourite ingredients, roll up and cook.

Starter SOS

You can't make a mother starter, you've 'killed' the starter, it no longer works, it smells strange, liquid has accumulated on the surface, the dough doesn't rise, you're going on holiday – there are so many questions about sourdough and its use in baking. All the answers are in this chapter. But let's proceed in order!

Mother starter, sourdough starter, sourdough, leaven, wild yeast – are you lost in a flood of names?

The mother starter, sometimes referred to as the sourdough starter or simply sourdough or starter, is the sourdough starter that you always have in the jar, your original starter, from which you take and always keep. The intermediate step in dough preparation is the leaven itself, for which you use some of your own starter. It has two functions: it allows you to check the work of your starter, and if you use a different flour in the dough, you use it to feed the starter. However, if you'll be using the same flour you normally use to feed your starter, just feed it well and make sure it is alive, that the bubbles burst and doubles in volume before using it in the dough. That's usually how I do it. My container has a capacity of 360 ml, I keep 40 g of starter in it, which I feed with a mixture of stone-ground organic wheat flour (50 per cent type 550/white plain and 50 per cent type 812/strong white). Before putting the container back in the fridge, I refresh it. When I take it out of the fridge, I add 40 g of water and 32 g of flour (80 per cent hydration). You can of course hydrate yours 100 per cent if you wish.

What utensils do I need for my mother starter?

A jar with a volume of 400 ml or less. It should be made of glass, because glass resists acid. You'll also need a mixing spoon – plastic, metal or wooden – kitchen scales, quality flour and non-chlorinated or water left standing overnight.

Which flour is suitable for making sourdough?

All flours are suitable, but to work with lactic acid bacteria and wild yeasts, it is preferable to use rye or wheat flour. Both varieties are packed with nutrients and minerals that activate lactic acid bacteria and yeasts more quickly. In addition, wholemeal flour contains many husks with multiple yeasts on them. Flour should be organic as far as possible, as plant-care products, especially fungicides, prevent the growth of these beneficial organisms. If possible, buy stone-ground flour or grind it yourself at home. With flour from the supermarket, the starter may take a little longer to start bubbling.

Which water should be used to prepare the starter, the leaven and the dough?

In my experience, I recommend filtered water or a jug with a carbon filter that removes chlorine. Chlorine has an antimicrobial effect that inhibits the growth of lactic acid bacteria and yeast. If you do not have such a jug, you can fill a container with water and leave it to stand for at least an hour, or better overnight, to allow the chlorine to evaporate. But you can also boil it and leave it to cool down. When the mother starter is strong enough, it will tolerate chlorinated water, but I prefer to use only filtered water. Test and judge for yourself!

I've started to prepare my mother starter, but after 2–3 days there is no activity, just a bubble here and there, and this is probably from stirring.

Don't let this get you down, it might be the room temperature may be too low, especially in winter. It can take a little longer for microorganisms to come alive and become active because they need a suitable environment, warmth, food (flour) and water. Check what flour you feed it and what water you use. Place the container in a warm, upright position, but not on a radiator or near a source of high heat. An acid smell is a good sign. If there is no mould, all is well and you can continue the procedure described on page 58. Time is a key factor in making a starter, as is patience. Don't give up, wait for bacteria and yeasts to become active. If, however, despite all the advice (on flour, water, temperature), there is still no sign of life in the container after ten days, you can use home-made kefir or add a teaspoon of honey to the flour-water mixture. Once the micro-organisms have started working on the flour-water mixture, feed the starter as explained, i.e. only with flour and water.

My sourdough starter is ready, what now? Do I have to feed it daily?

If you make bread every day or every other day, you can simply leave it on the kitchen worktop and feed it every day. If not, you can put it in the refrigerator without any problem. However, you must first feed it using less water than flour (about 70 to 80 per cent hydration for wheat or spelt flour). The mixture then thickens and looks like a softer dough. For example, if you have 5 g of starter in the jar, feed it with 20 g of flour (e.g. wheat flour) and 15 g of water. Stir with the handle of a spoon, clean the sides of the jar, leave it to rest for about 1 hour, then seal the lid completely and put it back in the refrigerator.

The activity of the starter is slowed down by low temperature and reduced water, but it is still alive – don't worry, it is very resistant! The next time you take it out of the refrigerator, refresh it with more flour and water than the amount in the jar to activate the lactic acid bacteria and wild yeasts. When the contents have doubled, you can use it for the dough or to make a leaven, if you use a different flour in the dough than in the leaven.

When can I begin to use the starter?

When the cycle of rising and falling is steady, at a steady pace; when it has doubled before starting to collapse. If it is ready after 4 days, you can use it. It probably won't be very vigorous yet, but the bread will still rise. Imagine a curve: the sourdough is at its lowest point before being fed. When you feed it, the microorganisms begin to digest the food (the flour) and the starter grows until it reaches its highest point. Then it slowly runs out of food and the contents of the jar begin to decline until it reaches the level it was at before it was refreshed. Sourdough should be used when it is at the top of the curve, or just before. You can put an elastic band around the jar to help see how it rises. Follow a cycle and note how long it takes to double.

What does a normal sourdough starter look like?

In general, it smells a bit like yoghurt, is milky, with a pleasant sweet smell, possibly slightly acidic. It rises and falls evenly. At the peak of the curve, there are some nice bubbles (if you are using wheat flour type 405, 550/white plain or 812/strong white). With rye flour, it is rather a compact mixture, even at 100 per cent hydration. If you feed it with rye flour or wholemeal flour, the starter will develop a slightly acidic odour and act faster, as these flour varieties are more nutritious. White flour slows down the activity of the starter, as does less water. I recommend that you not only observe the functioning and rising of the starter, but also smell it from time to time, for example after feeding it, when it has risen and is beginning to deflate. You will quickly notice that the smell changes, in addition to the appearance.

What should the room temperature be?

The optimal temperature for maintaining the starter is between 24-26°C/75–78°F. This is where yeasts and lactic acid bacteria work best. In winter, when it is cold, the yeasts also work more slowly. In the summer, however, yeasts can become shocked when temperatures are high. In this book, when I talk about room temperature, I mean temperatures between 21–24°C/69–75°F.

I have been feeding my starter with rye flour, but I want to make a bread with another type of flour: how do I make it?

If you no longer want to use rye flour, gradually feed the starter with another type of flour.

You can also make an intermediate step in the form of a leaven to check the activity of the mother starter and use the type of flour with which you wish to prepare the dough.

What should I do if the starter has become a little lazy and is no longer working as it used to or if it has become runny?

Feed the starter well, adding more flour and water than there is mixture in the jar. You can keep one tablespoon of the starter and then add 40 g of flour and 30 g of water. It is also possible to stimulate it with a little rye flour: my experience has shown that this helps. Repeat the process if necessary. It is not necessary to add fruit, honey or other ingredients, as this only adds unnecessary extra organisms that are not specific to flour. You can also take a larger amount of starter, use it for another recipe if it is not too acidic, and add more fresh flour and water to the rest (e.g. one tablespoon) in the jar than it contains.

The mother starter has a strange, unusual odour and brown liquid has accumulated on the surface. Why is this?

It's likely it has a strong sour smell and is not growing anymore. The liquid that has accumulated on the surface is alcohol, so it should be discarded. If the mother starter has a pungent, alcoholic or over-fermented odour, it is a sign that the microorganisms have consumed all the food and have acidified the sourdough. It's a problem that often occurs when temperatures are high, in summer or when it has not been used for a long time. Don't worry, take almost everything out of the jar, leave only 5-10 g of sourdough, refresh it (e.g. with 20 g flour and 20 g water) and leave it to rest. When it has doubled, feed it again with more flour and water than is in the jar. If it has not doubled after 12–24 hours and the contents of the jar still have a strong acid smell, take out more than half of the contents again and feed the rest with more flour and water. It should recover after two refreshments. Don't be discouraged; be patient, because it sometimes takes a little longer for the microorganisms to do their work.

From time to time (once a month), I clean the jar in which I keep the starter completely. Residues on the walls of the jar may also give off a sour smell when the jar is open, as these deposits can themselves become sour.

In this case, remove the starter, rinse and dry the jar, put it back into the container and feed it again.

What can you do in the summer when it is very hot and the starter or dough is unstable?

Reduce hydration and keep the water very cold. You can also use cold flour. You can add a pinch of salt to the starter, which slows down its activity. When preparing the leaven, use less starter; this also applies to the dough mixture.

And what about in winter when the temperatures are lower?

Use more starter for kneading, which should not be acidic but should still smell a bit like yoghurt. The water can also be warmer, up to 35°C/95°F. You can put the dough overnight in the oven with the door closed and the light on.

Why have black spots appeared on the surface of the starter?

Sourdough starter is a stable microsystem and, with good care (i.e. nutrition and hygiene), it even prevents the penetration of harmful organisms, as only certain good, specific yeasts thrive in an acidic environment. In the early stages of development, cross infection and mould may develop on the surface of the mother starter or on the sides of the glass jar. If the mould is black, discard the mother starter and start again with a new one.

Why does the sourdough starter smell like acetone/paint thinner?

It is a common phenomenon at high temperatures and with a wheat flour-based starter when not used frequently. Under these conditions, lactic acid bacteria can produce more acetic acid than usual, which is rapidly converted into acetone. If you refresh the starter with flour and water, the smell will disappear. Take 5 to 10 g of this starter and add at least 30 g of flour and 30 g of water. Leave the jar to stand and repeat the process if necessary.

What should I do if I need more starter than I have?

For example, you may only have 40 g of starter in the jar, but you need 300 g. Simply take, for example, 35 g of starter and add flour and water until you reach 300 g. The microorganisms will multiply. Feed the remaining 5 g starter in the jar, e.g. with 20 g flour and 15 g water, leave to rest for about 1 hour and then return the jar to the refrigerator.

How much starter should be used in the leaven and how much leaven should be used in the dough?

The amount depends on how fast your dough has to rise. In principle, you should use 10 to 30 per cent of your mother starter for the leaven and then 10 to 30 per cent of the leaven for the dough. Thus, for every 1 kg of flour, that makes 100 to 300 g of starter or leaven.

For my part, I take between 10 and 30 per cent, knowing that 2 heaped teaspoons of active starter-wheat flour mixture weighs about 30 g.

The smaller the quantity used, the slower the dough rises, and vice versa. It is better to use a lower percentage, as this allows the taste to develop slowly. Lactic acid bacteria need at least 12–24 hours to develop the aromatic compounds that improve the taste of bread.

How can I slightly accelerate the work of the starter/leaven?

When it's cold outside or I need a larger quantity quickly, I help myself from time to time by feeding the mother starter or leaven with hot water (up to 35°C/95°F) and placing the jar in the oven with the door closed and the light on – or by heating a cup of water in the microwave, then turning it off and putting my fed starter in it.

Do I need to add baker's yeast along with starter when making a dough?

No, because the active starter alone ensures the leavening of the dough. What's more, when adding yeast, it is impossible to use lactic fermentation, because lactic acid bacteria do not have time to do their job due to the rapid action of baker's yeast.

How much water is needed, e.g. for 500 grams of flour?

It depends on the flour you use. Rye flour absorbs more water than wheat flour, spelt flour less. For wheat flour you will start with a hydration of about 60 per cent, for rye flour with a hydration of 68–70 per cent and for spelt flour with a hydration of 55 per cent. Wholemeal flours also absorb more water than white flours because of the bran particles they contain. After autolysis, you will know exactly how much water the flour can still absorb, and you can then add more.

Do I have to knead the dough?

Kneading serves to strengthen the gluten network. If the gluten is strong, the bread also has a more open crumb, leavens better more easily and keeps its shape. Kneading is not necessarily essential, but without it, the bread will be smaller and the crumb will be more dense. If you knead by hand, knead the dough two or three times for 2–3 minutes each time. These times are given as an indication. If you use a food processor, take care not to knead the dough too much, otherwise the gluten will separate from the water.

Do I really have to make stretches and folds?

No, not necessarily. This technique is used to reinforce the gluten strands and redistribute nutrients as they increase. If you knead the dough well after autolysis, for example two or three times at 2–3-minute intervals, this will be sufficient. For more volume, better leavening and if you have enough time, knead the dough more.

I've been feeding the starter, but the bread does not rise or rises very slowly. Is something wrong?

Was the mother starter active and full of bubbles before the leaven was made? If you haven't used the sourdough for a long time and/or if it has been left in the refrigerator, feed it 6–12 hours before using it. Maybe the starter is too acidic? Feed it enough. Perhaps you used too little water for the dough? The less water you use, the slower the dough rises. The temperature also has a great influence on the rise. This is particularly evident during the change of seasons when temperatures drop. Any change, however small, can significantly prolong the process.

How do I know that the dough has risen enough to be baked?

Observe the change in volume of the dough and perform the finger test. Press a finger 1 or 2 cm deep into the dough. When the dough is just ready to bake, the hole closes slowly, but not completely. It's time to preheat the oven. In the meantime, you can put the dough in the refrigerator to firm up a little.

If the dough has not yet risen sufficiently, the hole will quickly close again, in which case you will have to wait a little longer before baking. If the depth of the hole is intact, the dough is over-fermented. Gluten strands can no longer retain carbon dioxide and start to degrade. But don't worry, just bake the dough, it will be good and tasty, even if it doesn't rise in the oven any more and collapses or falls apart a little.

Before baking, the dough spreads out, and it does not rise during baking. Why?

There can be several possible causes, or even a combination of them, but let's proceed in order.

One of the most common causes is too much water in the dough. Slowly add the water to the flour while stirring. Next time start with a smaller amount, after autolysis you can still add water.

You may have kneaded the dough too little and therefore the gluten network is underdeveloped. Knead longer next time. When gluten strands are strengthened enough, the flour will also absorb more water.

The first rise was too short and the dough could not be strengthened; leave it to rise slightly longer next time. Also use the stretch and fold technique.

You used a large percentage of wholemeal flour, which cuts the gluten strands because of the bran. For the next kneading, you can first soak the wholemeal flour, mix it with white plain or strong white flour and even more water after 1 hour, or use up to 50 per cent wholemeal flour. Spelt flour also contains weak gluten, which is stretchy but not elastic, and therefore tends to spread.

The amount of gluten-free flour used (e.g. maize, buckwheat) in the dough was too large, so the dough spreads out, as there was not enough structure to support it as it rises. Use no more than 30 per cent of this type of flour. You can also boil it. You may have used too many additives (seeds, grains, bran, flakes, etc.). All of these ingredients weaken the gluten network. Add them when you have already strengthened the dough. Always soak them overnight.

If you have added fruit or some vegetable puree to the dough, they may cause the dough to break even faster due to the enzymes it contains. Use a smaller amount or add this ingredient when you have already developed the gluten bonds.

The preshaping and final shaping were too feeble. Next time try to create more tension on the surface of the dough. You can also place the dough in a baking tin if you notice that it is very soft at this step.

The dough has risen too much. Think of the dough as a balloon: it can be inflated to some extent, then burst. If you notice that the dough has risen too much, shape and leave it to rise again, and then bake.

The final rise was too long, allowing the dough to ferment too much and the gluten bonds to begin breaking down. In this case, you can add more flour, water and salt to the dough, mix and leave to rise again. Note however the dough will rise faster this time. Leave to rise for a shorter time to the next bake, and don't forget the finger test.

Should I stick to the times indicated or should I rely on the dough?

When cooking with sourdough, it is certainly best to forget about the clock and instead watch how the dough behaves.

Therefore, all indications of duration given in this book should be considered as only an approximate guide. This does not mean, of course, that you have to wait next to the dough to monitor it, because wild yeast and lactic acid bacteria work slowly and need sufficient time. Use all your senses, observe the dough, touch it, feel it to see its changes.

Why does the dough break down when I try to shape it?

You let it rise and ferment for too long and the enzymes have broken down the protein/gluten, which is now breaking down. The dough gradually turned into a large piece of starter. You can try adding a little flour, water and salt and knead again. The dough will rise much faster this time, so you have to keep an eye on it.

The bread has very even holes but in some places a very closed firm crumb. There's a large hole under the crust. Why?

There are a number of possible reasons. Maybe your starter wasn't active enough. The bulk fermentation might have been too short, or even the final rise. The dough wasn't scored or wasn't scored deep enough or it was baked in a too hot oven with too little steam.

Why has the bread cracked along the side?

This may be due to a problem in the shaping. The dough didn't rise long enough. You didn't score it deep enough. The oven was too hot and not enough steam was used..

Why is the crust pale?

The baking temperature was too low. Too little steam at the beginning of the baking process. Too short or too long rising, the dough no longer contains enough sugar for the Maillard reaction and the colouring of the crust.

How do I know when the bread is baked?

The more bread you make, the better you can judge when to take it out of the oven. The crust should be uniformly brown and firm. You can check if the bread is sufficiently cooked simply by tapping on it. When it sounds hollow, it's cooked. You can also use a baking thermometer to check the inside temperature (about 95-100°C/203–212°F for bread and about 110°C/230°F for enriched dough). The approximate baking time per 1 kg of dough is 40–50 minutes.

Why is my wholemeal bread so flat with a closed/compact crumb?

Wholemeal flour contains a lot of bran (parts of the husks of the grains), which has sharp edges and can damage the gluten network, so that the gluten cannot form longer chains. I recommend that you mix the flours and add at least 30-50 per cent type 405, 500 (white plain) or 812 (strong white) wheat flour to the wholemeal flour. The bread will still taste very good, but the crumb will be more airy and softer.

The bread tastes bland, as if something is missing. It may also be pale. Why?

You may have forgotten to add salt.

What to do to make the bread more sour?

If you really like a sour taste, you can strengthen it by using the starter or leaven after it has started to deflate slightly for the premix with hot water (at 30-35°C/86-95°F). Then let the dough rise in a warm place (30-35°C/86–95°F). These temperatures are ideal for the development of lactic acid bacteria, which in turn produce more lactic acid and acetic acid. You can also place the dough in the refrigerator during the last proving, as low temperatures favour the formation of acetic acid.

What if I don't want my bread to be sour?

Use a fresh starter or leaven before it reaches its peak, i.e. before it slowly deflates and runs out of food. Refresh the starter several times so that it does not become too sour and thus stimulates the growth of wild yeasts. Make the dough with white flour; wholemeal flour ferments faster and the lactic acid bacteria will produce more acid. Do not use water that is too hot.

If your starter is very active and forms lots of bubbles, you can use more of it and the dough will rise faster. However, in this case the lactic acid bacteria may not be able to do all its work. It can be put into the refrigerator for the final rise.

How can I make bread with large holes?

The soft and juicy crumb with large holes depends on several factors. But, in principle, these larger holes can be obtained with appropriate flour (white, strong white, smaller amount of wholemeal), with more water in the dough if the flour can take it up, with properly developed gluten in the dough, with gentle handling in preshaping and the final shaping, with the right fermentation and slow and long rise in the refrigerator.

Despite planning, I've accumulated too much starter, what can I do?

You can find recipes for using excess starter in the chapter 'What If There's Too Much Starter' on pages 236–250. You can also use sourdough in absolutely any dish to improve the taste, thicken, etc. – there should be no limits to your imagination. For more ideas, see pages 250-251. You can also dry, grind and store it for all occasions.

How and where can flour be stored properly?

Personally, I store the flour in a dark, cool place. Since I usually buy it from organic farmers, I put it in the fridge for at least 2 days when I get home. If you grind the flour yourself at home, always try to grind it just before mixing and use it within 24 hours.

How can I store bread properly?

After slicing the bread, I lay the sliced end against the bread board for the first 2 days, and usually wrap it in a linen or cotton bread bag. After 2 days, I sometimes wrap it in a plastic bag over the linen bag to keep it from drying out. Because of the low temperatures, the refrigerator is not suitable for storing bread and, on the contrary, accelerates its ageing.

I won't be baking for a long time, or I'm going to be travelling and can't take the starter with me. What should I do?

If you know you will be away for a long period of time, you have several options. First of all, you can feed the starter well before you leave and sharply reduce the hydration (the amount of water) to 60–70 per cent (make a very hard dough), leave it to rest for 30 minutes–1 hour and then put it in the refrigerator. Because the starter will now contain less water, the lactic acid bacteria and yeasts it contains will also move more slowly and therefore digest nutrients more slowly.

You can also mix the starter with a lot of flour and make small pieces, which you can then keep in the refrigerator.

Once, I accidentally froze the starter myself, it survived a week's holiday in the corner of the freezer. When I got home, I first thawed it and after two refreshments, it was ready for work again. The longer it stays in the freezer, the more microorganisms die.

You can always create a dry base. When the sourdough is well, active and full of bubbles, spread it over silicone sheet or baking paper and leave it to dry in the open air or in an oven at 30-40°C/86–104°F. Then grind it to a powder. When you return, first dissolve this powder (e.g. 10 g) in water (30 g), then add rye flour or wholemeal flour (20 g) to make the starter work faster, and a little more water (20 g). During the next refreshment, increase the amount of flour and water, e.g. 30 g flour and 30 g water. After two refreshments, your mother starter should be alive again. If not, feed it again.

You can also ask someone to look after your mother starter and feed it while you are away. Prepare precise instructions in this case.

Personally, I never throw away a starter, even after a long absence, however, it can recover quite quickly. When I go, usually to a rental property, I take my sourdough starter with me so that I can enjoy fresh sourdough delights during the holidays.

If you have not found an answer to your question despite careful reading, I cordially invite you to join the first Slovenian Facebook group dedicated to sourdough baking, which I have named Drožomanija (Sourdough_Mania). You will be able to ask questions, ask for help and share your experiences of sourdough and your enthusiasm with other enthusiasts. You can also find me on Instagram at @sourdough_mania and on Anita Šumer's Facebook page (@sourdoughmania).

Baking
schedules

In this chapter you will find different scenarios that will help you to integrate sourdough baking into your daily routine. In the schedules, I refer to baking bread, but this also applies to other bakery products. If you place the shaped dough in the refrigerator, it can be kept for a day or two, except for rye and spelt flours, which ferment very quickly if not mixed with other types of flour. When beginning with sourdough, the main concern is usually how to organise the different stages of preparation.

Personally, I have discovered over time that the refrigerator is my best friend since I don't have to get up in the middle of the night to make bread or stay up late until the dough is ready to bake. (Although I've been doing it for a long time.) All the steps described in the first part of the book apply regardless of the cooking scenario.

Fresh bread for Sunday morning breakfast?

Take the mother starter out of the fridge on Friday night, feed it well or prepare a leaven. Leave it out all night to double in size. On the next morning or afternoon, knead the dough. Leave it to rise, covered, and preshape and final shape. Put the dough in a proving basket or loaf tin and leave it to stand in a warm place for 2–3 hours. Then put it into the refrigerator. On Sunday morning, check whether the dough has risen properly. If it has risen enough, bake it straight out of the fridge, otherwise prove it at room temperature.

Bread for dinner, like on Tuesday at the end of the day?

On Monday evening, take your starter out of the fridge and feed it well or prepare a leaven. Leave it to rest at room temperature overnight to double in size. Mix the dough ingredients on Tuesday morning, add a little starter or leaven and knead well.

Cover and leave it to rise in a warm place to have it ready for shaping when you get home from work. On your return, preshape and final shape the dough, leave it to rise in the loaf tin or basket and bake it in the oven Tuesday night, or early the next morning.

Bread for lunch, say Wednesday around 2 pm?

On Tuesday morning, take your starter out of the fridge and feed it well or prepare a leaven. Leave it to rest at room temperature to double in size until you return from work that afternoon. Then knead the dough, leave it to rise in a container with a lid, then preshape and final shape it on Tuesday night. You can then leave the dough at room temperature for 2–3 hours or refrigerate it and take it out early Wednesday morning to allow it to rise and double in size again before baking around 1 pm.

Bread for Friday afternoon after work?

On Thursday morning, take your starter out of the fridge and feed it well or prepare a leaven. Leave it to rise at room temperature to double in size until you return from work Thursday afternoon. Then knead the dough, leave it to rise in a container with a lid, then preshape and final shape it on Thursday night. Leave the dough at room temperature for 2–3 hours, then refrigerate until the next day. See how the dough has grown in the fridge on Friday morning, and leave it at room temperature for 1 hour if necessary. When you go to work, put it back in the fridge. When you return home, you can bake it if it is sufficiently risen, otherwise leave it at room temperature until ready for baking.

Glossary

Active starter – starter that been fed and doubled in size and is full of bubbles.

Autolysis – self-degradation, decomposition of the dough by its own enzymes.

Baking percentages – the basis for calculating quantities, see p. 46.

Bench knife – a special baker's knife used to cut the dough and help shape it.

Cast-iron casserole – cast-iron pot with a lid, suitable for baking bread, as it stores heat and accumulates moisture well.

Ceramic or fireclay baking stone – heat-resistant boards intended for baking bread products.

Feeding the starter – adding fresh flour and water to the starter.

Final prove – the last rise in the loaf tin or proving basket.

First rise – the rise in a bowl, covered, after kneading.

Lactic acid bacteria – microorganisms that cause lactic acid fermentation and are present in the yeast.

Hydration – the amount of water in the dough in relation to the amount of flour, see page 46.

Leaven – an intermediate stage with a sourdough starter.

Mother starter/sourdough starter/starter/sourdough – the one in the jar, which you feed and from which you take a certain amount for the preparation of the leaven; see pages 50–62.

Proving basket/banneton – a basket intended for the final rise of bread.

Scoring – a technique in which a bench knife or razor blade is used to cut the dough on the surface to allow steam to escape, to break through the crust and to define where the bread opens.

Steel plate, e.g. pizza steel – steel plate with good heat transfer qualities for baking bread products.

Stencil – a plastic or wooden device for creating patterns across the surface of the dough.

Stretch and fold – a technique by which the dough is strengthened after mixing. Part of the dough is stretched upwards and then folded forwards. This is repeated all around the bowl.

Wild yeasts – single-cell microorganisms, which are present in a starter and make the dough rise.

Bibliography

Bavec, F., 2000. Some neglected and/or new crops. Maribor: Faculty of Agriculture.

Bogataj, J., 2007. Tasting Slovenia. Ljubljana: Darila Rokus.

Dictionary of the Slovene Literary Language, www.fran.si, access 10. 8. 2017

Elezebroek, ATG, & Koop, W., 2008. *Guide to cultivated plants*. Cambridge: CABI.

Grobelnik Mlakar, S., 2012. Agronomic characteristics, potential use and quality grain kernel crop, doctoral thesis. Maribor: University of Maribor, Faculty of Agriculture and Biosystem Sciences.

Hadjiandreou, E., 2016. *How to Make Sourdough*. London: Ryland Peters & Small.

Hamelman, J., 2013. *Bread*. Hoboken, New Jersey: John Wiley & Sons Inc.

Hrovat, M., 2000. The technological basis of bread production. Ljubljana: Technical publishing house of Slovenia.

Hrovat, M., 2010. Milling (electronic source). Ljubljana: Biotechnical Education Centre.

Kocjan Ačko, D., 1999. Forgotten crops. Ljubljana: ČZD Kmečki glas.

Kocjan Ačko, D., 2015. Crops; production and use. Ljubljana: ČZD kmečki glas.

Kocjan Ačko, D., et al., 1998. Spelt, the new discovery of the forgotten grain. Ljubljana: Ministry of Agriculture, Forestry and Food.

Kreft, I., 1995. Buckwheat. Ljubljana: ČZD Kmečki glas.

Owens, S., 2015. *Sourdough*. Boulder: Roost Books.

Robertson, C., 2010. *Tartine Bread*. San Francisco: Chronicle Books LLC.

Tanjšek, T., et al., 1991. Corn. Ljubljana: ČZD Kmečki glas.

Todorič, I., and Gračan, R., 1982. Special farming. Ljubljana: State Publishing House of Slovenia.

Vombergar, B., el al., 2016. Proso - Millet. Ljubljana: ČZD Kmečki glas.

Whitley, A., 2017. *Do Sourdough – Slow Bread for Busy Lives*. London: The Do Book Company.

Wood, E., 1996. *World Sourdoughs from Antiquity*. Berkeley, California: Ten Speed Press.

Useful websites

www.sourdoughmania.com
www.questforsourdough.com
www.northwestsourdough.com
www.sourdough.co.uk
www.breadwerx.com

index

ANITA ŠUMER

Anita Šumer

info@drozomanija.si

www.sourdoughmania.com

Instagram: sourdough_mania

Facebook: Anita Šumer (sourdoughmania)
Facebook group: Drožomanija

YouTube: Sourdoughmania

SOURDOUGH_MANIA

NOTES

NOTES

This English language edition published in 2020 by
Grub Street
4 Rainham Close
London
SW11 6SS

Email: food@grubstreet.co.uk
Twitter: @grub_street
Facebook: Grub Street Publishing
Web: www.grubstreet.co.uk

Assistant: Sašo Šumer
Photographs: Primož Lavre
Design: Staša Filipi Tasič, Manca Zupanc
Styling: Polonca Klančnik, Barbara Remec
First published in Slovenian by ARS VERBI, Anita Šumer, s.p

A CIP record for this title is available from the British Library
ISBN 978-1-911621-93-5

Printed and bound in Poland by Hussar Books

DOUGH PREPARATION

KEY:

Ⓛ **TIMING**

❄ **CAN BE REFRIGERATED**

MAIN DOUGH / AUTOLYSIS

KNEADING
2–3 times at
2–3 minute interva[l]

water — flour

sourdough

20 min Ⓛ

❄

SHAPING

FINAL RISE

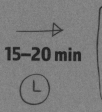

15–20 min Ⓛ

5 min Ⓛ